Collins

Get Ready for IELTS

IELTS

Teacher's Guide

Pre-intermediate to Intermediate
IELTS Band 3.5–4.5

Fiona McGarry
Patrick McMahon
Els Van Geyte
Rod Webb

William Collins' dream of knowledge for all began with the publication of his first book in 1819.

A self-educated mill worker, he not only enriched millions of lives, but also founded a flourishing publishing house. Today, staying true to this spirit, Collins books are packed with inspiration, innovation and practical expertise. They place you at the centre of a world of possibility and give you exactly what you need to explore it.

Collins. Freedom to teach.

HarperCollins*Publishers*
The News Building,
1 London Bridge Street
London SE1 9GF

First edition 2016

Reprint 10 9 8 7 6 5 4 3 2

© HarperCollins*Publishers* 2016

ISBN 978-0-00-813918-6

Collins® is a registered trademark of HarperCollins*Publishers* Ltd.

www.collinselt.com

A catalogue record for this book is available from the British Library

Authors: Fiona McGarry
         Patrick McMahon
         Els Van Geyte
Series editor: Rod Webb
Publisher: Celia Wigley
Commissioning editor: Lisa Todd
Editors: Michael Appleton, Helen Marsden
Audio: dsound
Cover design: Angela English
Typeset in India by Jouve
Printed in Italy by Grafica Veneta S.p.A

CONTENTS

Introduction

Welcome to Get Ready for IELTS!

This exam preparation course has been specially designed to help pre-intermediate students working in an IELTS band score of 3.5-4.5 to move up to an intermediate level so that they are ready for an IELTS preparation course.

The resources for students and teachers include:

- Student's Book with audio CD
- Workbook
- Online resources via Collins Connect, for both students and teachers
- this Teacher's Guide with audio CD

The course follows a flipped learning approach, in which students do pre-class preparation in order to maximise the usefulness of the time spent in class. According to Dr Paschalis Chliaras, writing in *IATEFL Voices*, Issue 244, two key features of the flipped learning approach are an increase in both students' motivation to prepare for class and their willingness to participate in class activities that encourage active learning. Here are the three steps to the *Get Ready for IELTS* flipped learning approach.

Using the flipped learning approach

STEP 1 Pre-class preparation

Students prepare for their IELTS class with the language development exercises in the online resources on Collins Connect. If your students do not have access to Collins Connect, these language development exercises can be done in the Workbook. By learning vocabulary and grammar in advance, students can focus on developing the key skills and exam strategies for passing the test in class.

STEP 2 Skills development

In class, students learn the skills they need for the exam through the *Develop your exam skills* exercises in the Student's Book. You can support your students as they work through the course.

STEP 3 Exam practice

Each unit in the Student's Book contains exam practice, which gives students the opportunity to practise the skills they have been developing by providing realistic exam practice. The format of the *Practice for the test* sections for each skill follows the actual exam and you can use this to check your students' progress towards being ready for the test. This part of the Student's Book can also be set as homework giving you further flexibility.

Resources for students

Online resources through Collins Connect

The online resources contain all the **pre-class preparation** work for students. The activities are self-marked, with a 'reveal' feature so that students can check their answers, making it easy for them to see what they have retained and what they need to work on. There is additional practice material with a focus on grammar, spelling, punctuation and sentence structure to help students prepare for the writing and speaking sections of the exam. You can access Collins Connect here: **www.collins.co.uk/connect**

Workbook

This contains all the **pre-class preparation** work for students and is an alternative to the online resources on Collins Connect. A **Punctuation guide** to help students improve their writing skills and exercises to help students avoid common errors are also included. The **audio** for this component is included on the Student's Book CD (and on the Teacher's Guide CD).

Student's Book

Each of the 12 units in *Get Ready for IELTS* is topic based and covers **common themes** that come up in the IELTS exam. The language in the units is carefully graded to help students improve the four **exam skills** assessed in the IELTS test: Listening, Reading, Speaking and Writing. Additionally, there are key grammar, vocabulary and pronunciation **exercises** in every unit that build language skills and improve accuracy. Two regular features in the Student's Book are the **Exam information** boxes containing explanations of what to expect in the exam and **Exam tip** boxes containing strategies for succeeding in the exam.

At the end of each of the skills sections, students are given the opportunity to do some realistic **exam practice** that allows them to implement the skills they have learned. This practice can also help you to assess your students' readiness for the exam, or for a higher level IELTS preparation course. This part can be done in class or given as homework depending on time. At this level, students may find the exam practice quite challenging and teachers should provide support and encouragement.

Audio for the Listening and Speaking exercises can be found on the accompanying CD. At the back of the book, the **Grammar guide** provides clear explanations and examples of key language in use. References to this section are included throughout the units and there are additional exercises for each of the grammar points on Collins Connect for students to work through. There is also a **Practice test** at the back of the book.

Resources for teachers

This guide provides:

- Clear and easy-to-follow **lesson plans**, explanations and instructions for getting the most out of classroom time
- **Spot check activities** that you can use to check that the students have understood and retained the vocabulary and grammar preparation they have done before class
- Notes on **typical mistakes** students make and how to correct them
- **Answers** to the Student's Book exercises within the lesson plans for easy reference
- **Model answers** for Writing and Speaking exercises
- **Audio** for the Listening and Speaking exercises on the accompanying CD
- **Photocopiable activities** to accompany the Spot checks are available online on Collins Connect
- **Audioscripts** for the Listening and Speaking exercises are also available on Collins Connect

Number of hours

The course contains approximately 40-50 hours of classroom material, with an additional 50 hours of material that can be offered as homework, or for consolidation or extension in class. This additional material provides a high degree of flexibility for all classroom situations.

We hope you and your students enjoy using this course to 'get ready' for an IELTS preparation course.

UNIT 1: FAMILY

Speaking: Talking about the family

Student preparation for this class: Have students complete the Online / Workbook language preparation exercises at home before the lesson begins.

Teacher preparation: If you have not met your students before, you may want to do the preparation material for this unit in class. Students can either do this in the Workbook, or if they do not have a Workbook, you can download these pages from *Get Ready for IELTS* online or photocopy them from the Workbook.

Online / Workbook language preparation

Focus: The purpose of these exercises is to introduce language for talking about family: words for family members; pronunciation of /ð/; vocabulary for describing people; possessive adjectives; description of family members.

Develop your exam skills (Student's Book p. 6)

Focus: These exercises focus on Part 1 of the Speaking test: Introduction and interview. Exercises 1 and 2 focus on understanding the examiner's instructions; Exercises 3–7 train students to practise speaking effectively, to assess their own performance and identify strategies for improvement.

If this is your first time with the class, explain how the flipped classroom works. Point out that students will normally do their own preparation for the class online or in their Workbooks. Be enthusiastic about the idea and encourage students to see how it will benefit them: they will enjoy their classes more if they come along with some knowledge of the topic as well as an understanding of the vocabulary and grammar. Then work through the exercises with the class.

Introduction

1   Introduce the Student's Book unit by getting students to talk about the pictures on pages 10 and 13 in pairs. Ask them to try to describe some of the different families they can see. Elicit descriptions from students as a class.

2   If students did the Online / Workbook preparation before the class, use one of the Spot checks to clarify their understanding. You can use the other Spot check at an appropriate time during the lesson. If they did the preparation in the class, you can use the two Spot checks whenever you feel appropriate in this lesson or the next.

Spot check 1

To check students' recall of adjectives for describing character, do the following activity.

1.   Ask students to write three sentences describing themselves using the adjectives in Exercise 6 in the Workbook or Online.

2.   Put students in groups of 5–6 and designate one member of each group to act as facilitator.

3.   Facilitators gather their group's sentences, shuffle them and, without giving away who wrote them, read the sentences aloud.

4.   The other group members listen and guess who wrote each sentence.

Spot check 2

To check students' recall of possessive adjectives, do the following activity.

1.   Write your own responses to the questions in Exercise 13 in the Workbook or Online on the board, leaving gaps in place of all of the possessive adjectives.

2.   Students work in pairs to fill in the gaps.

 ### Exercise 1: Completing the examiner's instructions

a)   Go over the Exam information in Section 1 of the Speaking test on page 6. Explain that Exercise 1 is a typical start to the Speaking test. Have students work in pairs to try to complete the gaps.

b)   Play the recording (track 01) and let students complete the exercise. When you check their answers, find out what they had guessed incorrectly. Encourage them to discuss why they had different answers. Point out that it is useful to reflect on what they do in the classroom as this will help them learn more quickly.

Answers
1 name   2 full name   3 identification   4 family   5 do
6 How   7 country   8 friends   9 live

 ### Exercise 2: Matching a question and answer

a)   Have students guess which question they will hear answered. Then play the recording (track 02).

b)   Elicit the question and then what they remember about the answer. Encourage students to guess what they are not sure about, pointing out once again that this is part of the process of learning.

Answer
What does your father do?

 ### Exercise 3: Assessing a students response

a)   Put students in pairs and get them to discuss the six ways of rating answers to exam questions. While they are talking, go round checking their understanding.

b) Elicit what students think of the answer they heard in the recording. Then play the recording (track 02) again and ask them to rate the answers. Encourage discussion during feedback.

Answers
1 Most is relevant, but some is not relevant: 'He's very kind to people.'
2 OK
3 at normal speed
4 relevant: doctor, helps, people, hospital; not relevant: kind to people
5 clear
6 no errors

Exercise 4: Writing notes
a) Help students with note-taking by showing them how to do it. Elicit information from different students and write their responses in note form on the board. Highlight which words are omitted in notes, particularly articles and prepositions. Refer students to the Grammar section: *Possessive pronouns and adjectives*.

b) Students write their own notes. Once they have finished, have them think about how they will use them to speak using full sentences.

Exercise 5: Asking and answering
Have students work in pairs to ask and answer the question. Listeners provide feedback using the six questions in Exercise 5. If they have mobile phones with recording facilities, have them record their responses.

> **Typical mistakes:** Students may have difficulty with the pronunciation of /ð/ in *father* and the pronunciation of the final *s* in words like *works* and *he's*. Some students may forget to use the indefinite article with occupations, e.g. *He is doctor*.

Exercise 6: Improving an answer
Give students a few minutes to identify and practise at least one way of improving their response. Then have them repeat their answer, recording it if possible. Ask them to listen to their first and second attempts and note any improvements. If they have Workbooks, they can refer to the vocabulary, pronunciation and grammar sections in the Speaking section.

Exercise 7: Talking freely
a) Highlight the Exam tip. Emphasize how important it is for students to feel free to talk about anything as long as it is relevant. Point out that if they would prefer not to give real information about their family, they can invent information. This is a useful strategy if they don't know the words to explain something about their family.

b) Have students practise answering one other question from Exercise 1 following the same procedure.

Extension activity (10–15 mins)
To provide further practice in answering Speaking test Part 1 questions, do the following activity.

1. Ask each student to come up with as many questions as they can for one of the following topics: your country, your family, your hobbies, your studies or your work.

2. Have students stand up and circulate, asking each other their questions. Instruct them to change partners every minute.

 ## Practice for the test (20–30 mins)

This can be done in class as pairwork or assigned for homework. Remind students to look back at the Exam tips in the unit. Point out that students can do more activities online if they want extra practice or to consolidate what they have learnt.

Exercise 1
Model answer
1 I'm from Dubai. It's in the United Arab Emirates.
2 No, it's a small family. I'm an only child. There's just me, my parents and my grandmother.
3 My mother is a manager in an office.
4 Yes, we live in a big flat in the centre of the city.

Exercise 2
Questions
What do you do?
How would you describe your family?
Who is important to you in your family?

Model answers
1 I'm a teacher. I work in a language school.
2 My family is large. I have got two brothers and three sisters. My parents have got lots of brothers and sisters too.
3 My father is important to me. He works every day, but he always helps me with my studies. We like going for walks together.

Listening: A presentation about the family

> **Student preparation for this class:** Have students complete the Online / Workbook vocabulary preparation exercises at home before the lesson begins.
>
> **Teacher preparation:** If your students are not using a Workbook, you will need to download and print out the Spot check showing stress patterns within words.

Online / Workbook vocabulary preparation

> **Focus:** The purpose of these exercises is to introduce vocabulary relating to academic presentations; train students to recognize word stress and parts of speech; practise sorting words into vocabulary groups.

Develop your exam skills (Student's Book p. 8)

Focus: These exercises focus on Section 3 of the Listening test. They train students to identify future plans and stages in a presentation. Students practise answering a variety of question types: multiple-choice, note completion, labelling a diagram and sentence completion.

Introduction

Use one of the Spot checks to clarify students' understanding of the Online / Workbook vocabulary preparation. You can use the other Spot check at an appropriate time during the lesson.

Spot check 1

To reinforce students' awareness of word stress and how it relates to parts of speech, ask them to work in pairs and look at the answer key to Exercise 2 in the Workbook (or the Spot check handout) and try to identify any patterns.

(Possible answers: nouns ending in *-tion* are stressed on the penultimate syllable. Two-syllable verbs are often stressed on the last syllable, e.g. pre*sent*; two-syllable nouns are often stressed on the first syllable, e.g. *present*.)

Spot check 2

To reinforce how to learn words in vocabulary groups, do the following activity.

1. Ask each student to come up with a word (any word) and either write it on the board themselves or say it aloud for you to write.

2. Have students work in groups of three to sort the words into categories.

Exercise 1: Answering multiple-choice questions

a) Go over the Exam information on page 8 and the Exam tips. Highlight the importance of identifying the names of individual speakers as this then makes it much easier to identify what each one is saying, their opinions, etc. Ask follow-up questions about the second Exam tip, e.g.

    What makes multiple-choice questions difficult?

    What strategies can you use to help?

b) Introduce the topic of the recording. Point out that group presentations are common in academic study. Ask:

    Have you ever had to prepare a group project?

    What do you have to do to prepare a presentation?

c) Give students a minute to read the questions. Then play the recording (track 04) and check answers. You may want to refer students to the Grammar section: *Talking about future arrangements.*

Typical mistakes: Sometimes students choose an incorrect option (e.g. for question 3, they may choose b or c) because they have not waited for the negotiation to be completed. Explain that in this

---

section of the test, speakers often discuss several options before making a decision.

Follow up by giving students additional practice in following a conversation involving several speakers. Have students work in groups of five. Ask one student in each group to close their eyes and listen. Instruct the remaining members to swap seats and talk about an everyday topic of their choice. After a few minutes, the listener reports who said what.

Answers

1 b **2** b **3** a **4** b

Exercise 2: Completing notes

a) Highlight the instruction to write no more than two words or a number. Give students a minute to read the notes and predict the kind of words they will hear.

b) Play the recording (track 05). Pair students up to check their answers.

Answers

1 a comparison **2** 8 / eight **3** similar **4** different

Exercise 3: Labelling a slide

Follow a similar procedure to the one in Exercise 2.

Typical mistakes: If students have used more than two words for any of the gaps (e.g. for gap number 2: *blue bullet points*), remind them to follow the instructions exactly and cross out extra words.

Answers

1 title box **2** bullet points **3** image(s)

Exercise 4: Choosing multiple answers

a) Draw students' attention to the Exam tip. Then give them a minute to read the options in Exercise 4.

b) Play the recording (track 07) and have them complete the exercise.

Answers

a, e

Extension activity (60 mins)

This activity can be assigned for homework. Ask students to work individually or in small groups to prepare a presentation about families. In the next class, have students present their information informally to each other. If they have access to PowerPoint and a laptop, have them create some slides for their presentation.

Practice for the test (30 mins)

This can be done in class as pairwork or assigned for homework. Remind students to look back at the Exam tips in the unit. Point out that students can do more activities online if they want extra practice or to consolidate what they have learnt.

Answers

<u>Section 3</u>
1 b 2 c 3 b 4 b 5 Advantages 6 Accidents
7 Suggestions 8 7 / seven minutes 9 2 / two minutes
10 same style

Reading: Family structures

Student preparation for this class: Have students complete the Online / Workbook vocabulary preparation exercises at home before the lesson begins.

Teacher preparation: Download and print out Spot check definitions and answer cards. Then cut up as shown. You will need one set of cards and definitions per group of four. (15 mins)

Online / Workbook vocabulary preparation

Focus: The purpose of these exercises is to introduce words to talk about families and family structures.

Develop your exam skills (Student's Book p. 10)

Focus: These exercises introduce students to answering *True / False / Not Given* questions and help them develop their reading speed.

Introduction

Use the Spot check to clarify students' understanding of the Online / Workbook vocabulary preparation.

Spot check
To reinforce vocabulary related to the family, do the following activity.
1. Put students in teams of four.
2. Place the set of cards with the definitions of the words from the Online / Workbook vocabulary preparation in front of one team, face up. Place the set of cards with the words in front of another team, face up.
3. One team starts by reading out their first definition. The other team chooses the appropriate word or phrase from the cards in front of them. If it is correct, they turn the card face down; if it is incorrect, the other team takes the card from them.
4. The 'definition' team then reads out their next definition and the game continues until all twelve definitions have been used.
5. Any cards that have been 'taken hostage' by the opposing team have to be defined in order to be kept: the teams swap their lists of definitions and each team attempts to define their 'hostage' cards. If they cannot do this, they have to hand them back. The team with the most cards at the end of the game wins.
Note: If there is any disagreement about whether a definition is correct, the teacher's decision is final.

Exercise 1: Answering *True / Not given* questions

a) Go over the Exam information on *True/False/Not Given* answers. Highlight to students the importance of using information from the text and <u>not</u> making use of their own knowledge. Emphasize that this is a <u>reading</u> exercise.

b) This exercise raises awareness of when it is necessary to choose the option NOT GIVEN; there are no false options. It will be helpful if you remind students of this type of activity throughout the course.

c) Ask students to do the exercise individually and then compare their answers in pairs. During feedback, talk about which questions give full information and which ones involve speculation. You may then want to refer students to the Grammar section: *Direct and indirect questions in the present and past*.

Answers
1 ✓ 2 NOT GIVEN 3 NOT GIVEN 4 ✓ 5 NOT GIVEN
6 ✓

Exercise 2: Answering *True/False/Not given* questions

a) Have students do the exercise following the instructions in the book and then compare their answers in pairs. Explain that this exercise is preparation for the timed reading task in Exercise 3.

b) Deal with any issues that arise during class feedback. Refer to the Grammar section: *Talking about habits and ongoing situations*.

> **Typical mistakes:** Students may find this type of question difficult if they don't read the question carefully enough. It is important to read every word in the question and to pay attention to key words such as *sometimes, always, never, all, some, may, must*, etc. to ensure full understanding.

Answers
1 FALSE 2 TRUE 3 NOT GIVEN 4 NOT GIVEN
5 NOT GIVEN 6 TRUE 7 NOT GIVEN 8 TRUE
9 FALSE

Exercise 3: Talk about family structures

a) Have students work in groups and discuss what they have learnt about families in different cultures. Point out that it is important to take an interest in the information they read in the exam questions as it will help them understand the topic better and answer future questions.

b) Ask a few questions about the information in Exercises 1 and 2, e.g.

What is a nuclear family?

What are the advantages of having many brothers and sisters?

Exercise 4: Skimming and scanning

a) Focus on the Exam tip and have students read about skimming and scanning. Elicit the difference and discuss why these techniques are important.

b) Have students read Part 1 of the text using one of the techniques and then answer the questions. Point out that for these questions it is useful to scan for the words for parts of the world, e.g. *North America and northern Europe* and *other parts of the world*. Having found these phrases, students might need to read in detail.

c) Students then do the same for Part 2. Have them compare answers and discuss any improvement in their reading speed for Part 2. Ask them about what prevents them reading quickly; a common problem is reading sentences or sections twice. Share ideas on what helps students read faster.

> **Typical mistakes:** Students may spend too long on this type of question because they waste time searching for information. If the question refers to a topic or opinion that they did not notice when they skimmed the text and that they cannot find when they scan, the answer is probably *Not Given*.

Answers
Part 1
Paragraph 1: TRUE   Paragraph 2: FALSE
Paragraph 3: FALSE

Part 2
Paragraph 1: FALSE   Paragraph 2: TRUE
Paragraph 3: NOT GIVEN

Extension activity (40 mins)
To provide further practice in answering *True / False / Not Given* questions, have students write similar questions for each other.

1. Put students in groups of 3–4 and have them look at one of the texts in **Practice for the test** in Units 2–10 (a different text for each group).

2. Have students read their text and devise multiple-choice questions, one question for each paragraph. They should think carefully about the wording of each question.

3. Have groups swap reading texts and questions. See which group can correctly answer all the questions fastest.

Practice for the test (30 mins)

This can be done in class as pairwork or assigned for homework. Remind students to look back at the Exam tips in the unit. Point out that students can do more activities online if they want extra practice or to consolidate what they have learnt.

Answers
1 TRUE   2 NOT GIVEN   3 NOT GIVEN   4 FALSE
5 TRUE   6 FALSE   7 TRUE   8 TRUE

Writing: Family and society

> **Student preparation for this class:** Have students complete the Online / Workbook language preparation exercises at home before the lesson begins.
>
> **Teacher preparation:** Download and photocopy the Spot check 2 handout and cut out the modal verbs and sentences. Make one set for each group of 3–4 students. (15 mins)

Online / Workbook language preparation

> **Focus:** The purpose of these exercises is to practise spelling words for family relationships; introduce a range of modals; introduce the use of modals to indicate strength of opinion.

Develop your exam skills (Student's Book p. 13)

> **Focus:** These exercises continue the focus on writing a Task 2 essay. Exercises 1–3 provide information about the structure of individual paragraphs and practice in writing them; Exercises 4–6 provide practice in structuring multiple paragraphs within an essay.

Introduction
Use one of the Spot checks to clarify students' understanding of the Online / Workbook language preparation. You can use the other Spot check at an appropriate time during the lesson.

Spot check 1
To check students' ability to recall and spell words for family relationships, do the following activity.

1. Write the eight words from Exercise 1 in the Workbook or Online on the board with gaps as follows:

   *mo t _ _ _, d _ _ _ _ ter, _ _ _ ndm _ _ _ er, f _ t h _ _ - in-l _ _, gr _ _ ds _ n, _ ath_ _, _ _ n, p _ r _ _ t_*

2. Give definitions of the words in random order, e.g. *the mother of your parents, your father's wife.* Students respond by completing the words.

3. Ask students to use the words on the board to make four more words for family relationships, e.g. *father-in-law – parents-in-law, grandfather – granddaughter*.

4. Put students in groups of 3–4. Have them tell each other names of family members using the language in Exercise 1, e.g. *My grandmother's name is Lara*.

Spot check 2
To check students' understanding of the use of modal verbs to express possibility, necessity and opinion do the following activity.

1. Put students in groups of 3–4. Give one set of the Spot check 2 handout (cards with modal verbs and cards with sentences) to each group.

2. Groups match all six modals to the sentences – only one option will allow all the cards to be

used. (Answers: **1** should **2** might **3** don't need to **4** mustn't **5** need to **6** will)

3. Encourage groups to discuss different options and clarify any issues during feedback, e.g. a student might say: *My friend's young children <u>will</u> go to university* rather than *<u>might</u> go*. There is also a fine difference between the use of *should* and *need to*: *should* is a general obligation while *need to* implies that something is necessary in order to have a good outcome.

Exercise 1: Understanding the structure of a paragraph

a) Read the Exam information to students clarifying anything you feel necessary as you read. Ask students why it is important to follow a standard structure. Point out that to succeed in IELTS, they must do what the examiners require.

b) Ask students to read the example of a good paragraph, ignoring the underlined phrases, and answer the question. They should think about whether they agree or disagree with the author. Elicit opinions. Refer to the Grammar section: *Talking about possibility.*

c) Ask: *What might happen to children who don't have love and support from their parents?*

Have students find an example in the text. Then have them identify the three underlined parts of the text and the function of each one.

d) Have students work in pairs and answer the *True / False* questions.

Exercise 2: Showing understanding of paragraph structure

Have students answer the six *True / False* questions to check their understanding of paragraph structure. Deal with any issues that arise.

Answers
1 F 2 T 3 T 4 F 5 F 6 T

Exercise 3: Assessing two paragraphs

a) Ask students to work individually and decide which paragraph follows the rules in Exercise 1. Tell them to put a tick against anything that follows the rules and a cross against anything that breaks the rules.

b) Have students check their answers in pairs. Highlight the phrase at the beginning of Paragraph C: *Rules are important* [for children]. Prompt students to produce different ways of saying this and write their ideas on the board, e.g.

Children need (to be taught) rules.

Parents should teach their children rules.

It is important for children to have rules.

Refer to the Grammar section: *Modal verbs for ability* and *First conditional for possibility.*

Answers
Paragraph A follows the rules in Exercise 1.
Paragraph B uses definite language, e.g. *children will be really terrible, rules must be taught.* The sentence containing the main idea is at the end of the paragraph.

Paragraph C contains more than one main idea (rules, beliefs and social skills) and the ideas supporting the main idea aren't clear.

Exercise 4: Beginning a paragraph

a) Go through the Exam tip. Give students a few minutes to discuss whether this advice follows on from what they learnt in Exercises 1 and 2.

b) Introduce Exercise 4 by pointing out that each sentence can start with an opinion like the ones you wrote on the board after Exercise 3. Have students read the first paragraph to see how the first sentence summarizes it.

c) Students complete paragraphs 2–4 in the same way and then check their answers in pairs.

Suggested answers
2 Women should stay at home to care for the children and home.
3 It is important for children to grow up with brothers and sisters. / Parents should have more than one child.
4 Children should not help with housework.

Exercise 5: Ordering paragraphs

a) Students read the essay title. Check their understanding of what it is asking them to do.

b) Draw attention to the Exam tip. Point out that this will help them identify the introduction. Before they do the exercise, tell students to think clearly about the reasons for their choice and be ready to explain them. They then do the exercise individually and check their answers in pairs.

> **Typical mistakes:** Students often fail to follow advice on writing essays. For example, they may have a very short or weak conclusion because they don't see it as important, or they may simply repeat what they wrote in the introduction. This might be because writing follows a different style in their own culture, because their teacher has told them something different, or simply because they want to make their essay more interesting. Make it clear that they will only get a good mark if they follow the standard procedure for writing.

Answers
Paragraph 1: c   Paragraph 2: d   Paragraph 3: b
Paragraph 4: a

Exercises 6: Matching definitions of paragraph functions

a) Tell students to think carefully about the definitions of different paragraph functions while doing the exercise. They can then use some of the language themselves when checking in pairs.

b) Do feedback as a class to provide a further opportunity to use the language of explanation.

Answers
1 Introduction: a   **2** Main body: c   **3** Conclusion: b

Extension activity (30 mins)

Have students look back at an essay they have already written and see if it can be divided into paragraphs in the same way as the structure they have looked at. Alternatively, use one essay that a student has already written that would be suitable for such a task and have all students work on it.

Practice for the test (60 mins)

This can be done in class or assigned for homework. Suggest that students spend up to 60 minutes on the task to allow them to develop the skills they need to produce good quality work. As students become more proficient, the amount of time they spend on practice exam tasks can be gradually reduced until they can complete the work within the time allotted in the exam.

Task 2
Model answer
Some people say that children should always follow their parents' advice; others claim that this is not always right. I believe that children should follow their parents' advice when they are young, but they should become more independent when they are older.

Young children do not know the difference between right and wrong, and a parent is the best person to teach them this. For example, young children do not know that it is wrong to take things that do not belong to them. Parents can also teach children about dangers, both in the home and outside.

However, when children grow older, they should pay less attention to their parents. This is because parents might tell a child which career to choose, and this should be the child's decision. Parents sometimes want to tell their children how to live, but when they are grown up, they can decide for themselves. If a child doesn't make their own decisions, they might grow up to be less independent and strong. In conclusion, parents need to give young children advice on morals and safety, but not on how to live when they are older.

Listening: Hobbies, sports and interests

Student preparation for this class: Have students complete the Online / Workbook vocabulary preparation exercises at home before the lesson begins.

Teacher preparation: For the vocabulary Spot check, create cards with vocabulary items from Exercises 1 and 2 written on them (one item per card), sufficient for students to work in groups of three. See Spot check 1 and Spot check 2 for more information. (15 mins)

Online / Workbook vocabulary preparation

Focus: The purpose of the exercises is to introduce vocabulary related to hobbies, interests and sport: listening to activities with a focus on spelling; identifying words which sound the same but are spelt differently.

Develop your exam skills (Student's Book p. 16)

Focus: These exercises train students to complete a table and a form for the Listening test; they also focus on the differences in pronunciation between *l* and *r*, and *p* and *b*.

Introduction

1   Introduce the unit by getting students to talk about the pictures on pages 19 and 22 in pairs. Ask them to discuss what they can see and how it relates to the unit topic of *Leisure* and the Listening section *Hobbies, sport and interests*. Elicit information from students and clarify the difference in meaning between *hobbies*, *sport* and *interests*.

2   Use one of the Spot checks to clarify students' understanding of the Online / Workbook vocabulary preparation. You can use the other Spot check at an appropriate time during the lesson.

Spot check 1

To reinforce the vocabulary related to hobbies, interests and sports, have students talk about the ones that they like and dislike.

1.   Review or pre-teach sentence stems for talking about likes and dislikes, e.g. *I'm really keen on …, I find … fun / exciting / boring*.

2.   Put students in groups of three. Place face down one set of cards with the hobbies / interests / sports vocabulary on them.

3.   Players take it in turns to pick a card and make a full sentence that includes the name of the activity and whether they like it or not, e.g. *I'm not very keen on listening to music*.

4.   Monitor the activity, making a note of mistakes you hear.

5.   Write mistakes you heard on the board without saying who made them and put students in pairs to get them to correct the mistakes.

6.   Check the corrections with the whole class.

Spot check 2

To reinforce the terms *hobby*, *interest* and *sport*, play 'snap' with the same cards you used in Spot check 1.

1.   Review the words *hobby*, *interest* and *sport*. Put students in groups of three. Place face down one set of cards with the hobbies / interest / sports vocabulary on them.

2.   Students take it in turns to pick a card and turn it over quickly, putting it face up on the table so everyone can see it.

3.   Students immediately say one of the three words (*hobby*, *interest* or *sport*) that is appropriate to the word.

4.   The student who says the correct word first keeps the card. Play continues.

5.   The student with the most cards at the end wins.

 ### Exercise 1: Words with similar sounds

a)   Draw students' attention to the Exam tip. Write the words *right* and *light* on the board next to each other and say them aloud, pointing to each one as you do so. Do the same for *pat* and *bat*.

b)   Let students look at the pairs of words in Exercise 1 and have them say the words quietly to themselves to prepare them to hear the difference.

c)   Play the recording (track 11) twice before letting them compare their answers in pairs.

Typical mistakes: Students may still find it difficult to hear the difference between *l* and *r*, and *p* and *b*. If they need more practice, put them in pairs to say the words in Exercise 1 to each other. One student says one of the words while the other student listens and then points to the word that their partner is saying.

Answers
1 fry   **2** pray   **3** lead   **4** blade   **5** correct   **6** play
7 read   **8** fly   **9** played   **10** collect

 ### Exercise 2: Identifying words in conversations

a)   Ask students to guess which words in item 1 might be heard in the context of hobbies, e.g. *flying* could be heard in connection with flying a plane, *frying* in connection with cooking. Remind them that they should always try to predict what they are going to hear.

b)   Play the recording (track 12) and let them compare their answers in pairs.

Answers
1 flying   2 play   3 leading

Exercise 3: Understanding a table

a)   If you feel students would find it difficult to discuss what kind of stamps a collector might look for, you can do this as a class.

b)   Draw students' attention to the Exam tip. By following the advice in the tip, they will be able to predict the general topic of the recording, as well as the specific information that they will have to listen for. When they have done this, allow students to feed back their ideas as a class.

Answers
1 number   3 date   4 name of country

Exercise 4: Completing a table

a)   Play the recording (track 13) and let students compare their answers in pairs.

b)   Have students think about how the strategy in the Exam tip helped them to listen. It is important to give them an opportunity to reflect on the strategies they are learning.

Answers
1 1998   2 (the) USA / (the) United States   3 1967
4 Brazil

Exercise 5: Before listening

a)   Draw students' attention to the Exam tip and give them time to read the questions.

b)   Students then write notes about the type of information they are listening for and compare their notes in pairs.

> **Typical mistakes:** Students may need to write a name that will be spelt out for them when they complete a form and many students confuse letters. Here are some that are commonly confused and that you might want to give extra practice on: *G* and *J*, *E* and *I*, *A* and *H*, *M* and *N*, *O* and *U*.

Answers
2 address   3 name / spelling   4 phone number
5 personal / medical information   6 personal history

Exercise 6: Completing an application form

a)   Give students time to look at the form. Clarify the meaning of *previous experience*.

b)   Play the recording (track 14). Ask students to compare their answers in pairs.

Answers
1 Andrew Metcalfe   2 21   3 43A   4 571324   5 some

Extension activity (20 mins)
To provide further practice in listening and completing forms, have students work in pairs to role-play a similar

dialogue to the one in Exercise 6 using the form in the Student's Book.

1.   Tell students that they will role-play an applicant and an administrator of a climbing club.

2.   Put students in pairs and make one of them the administrator (the form filler) and one of them the applicant who wants to join the club.

3.   Have students prepare for the role play. The applicant should prepare some (invented) personal information, and the administrator should prepare questions to get the information required to fill in the form.

4.   Let students do the role play. Monitor.

5.   Have students swap roles and do the role play again.

 ### Practice for the test (30 mins)

This can be done in class as pairwork or assigned for homework. Remind students to look back at the Exam tips in the unit. Point out that they can do more activities online if they want extra practice or to consolidate what they have learnt.

Answers
1 table tennis   2 100   3 12   4 street dance
5–7 (in any order) b, e, g   8 Mandeville   9 Bury Gardens
10 07942573279

Speaking: How we relax

> **Student preparation for this class:** Have students complete the Online / Workbook language preparation exercises at home before the lesson begins.
>
> **Teacher preparation:** Photocopy handouts for Spot check 1 and cut into individual images. Do the same for the Spot check 2 handout. Make sufficient sets of each handout for students to work in groups of four. (25 mins)

Online / Workbook language preparation

> **Focus:** These exercises introduce language for talking about leisure activities: introducing phrases and verb-noun collocations associated with leisure activities; introducing adjectives; focusing on expressing preferences; reviewing the present simple tense.

Develop your exam skills (Student's Book p. 19)

> **Focus:** These exercises focus on Part 2 of the Speaking test: Individual long turn. Exercises 1–3 focus on understanding the examiner's instructions and the task card; Exercises 4–5 train students to prepare their response.

Introduction
Use one of the Spot checks to clarify students' understanding of the Online / Workbook language preparation. You can use the other Spot check at an appropriate time during the lesson.

Spot check 1

Check students' recall of leisure-related verb–noun collocations and vocabulary for expressing preferences.

1. On the board write the following expressions: *doing nothing, going for walks, playing computer games, reading magazines* and *using the Internet*.

2. Put students in groups of four and designate one member of each group to act as facilitator.

3. Place face down in front of each group images from the Spot check 1 handout.

4. The three speakers in each group take turns to pick the top card and say whether they like or dislike the activity using one of the phrases on the board and the correct verb–noun collocation (if necessary), e.g. *I love going shopping*.

5. The facilitators monitor accuracy.

Spot check 2

Check students' use of the present simple tense.

1. Keep students in the same groups of four but designate another person in each group to act as facilitator.

2. Shuffle and distribute one set of cards with the personal pronouns to each group.

3. The three speakers in each group take turns to pick an image card and a pronoun card and make a sentence using the present simple tense and a time expression: *on* + day, *at* + time, *at + the weekend*, *every* (*Tuesday*). If the pronoun card has a (+), the sentence should be in the affirmative, e.g. *She plays football every Saturday*. If the card has a (–), the sentence should be negative, e.g. *I don't watch TV on Sundays*.

4. Facilitators monitor accuracy.

 Exercise 1: Reading and understanding a task card

a) Go over the Exam information on Part 2 of the Speaking test. Students read the task card and discuss in pairs whether they would find it difficult or not. Deal with any issues that arise from the discussion as a class.

b) Play the recording (track 18). Give students a few minutes to discuss how they feel about doing this part of the exam.

Exercise 2: Identifying key words

a) Go over the Exam tip and clarify why it is useful to identify key words.

b) Students listen to the recording (track 19) and do the exercise. Let them compare their answers in pairs.

Answers
1 magazine   2 sport   3 interviews, news   4 the weekend   5 home   6 It's very interesting.

 Exercise 3: Matching students' answers to key words

a) Students try to do the exercise without listening to the recording.

b) Play the recording again and let them check their answers.

c) Invite students to suggest follow-up questions the examiner might ask, e.g. *Who are your favourite players* and *Why do you like them?*

Answers
1 newspaper or magazine   2 which parts   3 when   4 what kind   5 explain why   6 where

Exercise 4: Making notes for students' own answers

Students make their own notes for answering the task card questions in Exercise 1. Let them discuss their notes in pairs. Go round the class while they do this, offering any help they need.

Typical mistakes: Make sure that students do not write whole sentences at this stage. Encourage them to write one or two key words for part of the question. Point out that in the actual exam they will not have time to write whole sentences.

Exercise 5: Expanding notes into possible answers

a) Highlight the Exam tip and emphasize the importance of sticking to the time allocated for their answers.

b) Have students work individually to expand their notes into sentences.

Typical mistakes: Check that students use the gerund after verbs such as *enjoy* and *prefer*.

 ## Practice for the test (20–30 mins)

This can be done in class as pairwork or assigned for homework. Remind students to look back at the Exam tips in the unit. Point out that students can do more activities online if they want extra practice or to consolidate what they have learnt.

Answers
Exercise 1
Key words: activity, like, where, when, who with, why

Exercise 2 (Model answers)
Activity: watching DVDs
Where: home or at brother's flat
When: every weekend
Who with: my family
Why: relaxing, spend time with my family, eating

Exercise 3
Model answer
The activity I like doing is watching DVDs. I love watching films. I watch DVDs every weekend and sometimes in the week. I prefer watching films at home to going to the cinema. I watch films at my brother's flat too. I like watching films with my family. We cook a meal and then

we enjoy eating and watching a funny film. It's fun and I like spending time with my family.

Reading: Spending time with friends

Student preparation for this class: Have students complete the Online / Workbook vocabulary preparation exercises at home before the lesson begins.

Teacher preparation: None

Online / Workbook vocabulary preparation

Focus: The purpose of these exercises is to introduce the gerund, common words and verb-noun collocations associated with leisure time, and provide practice in working out the meaning of words from context.

Develop your exam skills (Student's Book p. 21)

Focus: These exercises train students to answer multiple-choice questions.

Introduction

Use the Spot check to clarify students' understanding of the Online / Workbook vocabulary preparation.

Spot check
To reinforce verb-noun collocations for leisure activities, do the activity below.

1. Put students in groups of five or six and designate one member of each group to act as facilitator.
2. On a blank sheet of paper, each student copies and completes the following sentence stems using the collocations listed in Exercise 3 of the Workbook or Online:

   My three favourite activities are …

   My three least favourite activities are …
3. Facilitators get together and without indicating names read aloud their group's responses.
4. The other group members listen and guess who wrote which responses.

Exercise 1: Reading for general understanding

a) Go over the Exam information on multiple-choice questions. Give students a few minutes to discuss what they find difficult about multiple-choice questions and the strategies they use to answer them.

b) Briefly discuss the question *How important is friendship for teenagers?* and elicit students' own opinions.

c) Have students read the text and answer the question. Encourage them to read quickly. (Note that there is more on reading skills in Unit 3.)

Exercise 2: Checking understanding of the text

a) Have students try to answer the question without re-reading the text. Then ask them to read the answer at the end of page 23.

b) As you check the answer, ask them to explain why options a–c are incorrect. This will help them learn to recognize common pitfalls.

Typical mistakes: Students may pick (b) or (c) because they are superficially similar to key phrases in the text, e.g. the expressions *computer gadgets* and *relationships with people* also appear in the text. Remind them to focus on the meaning of the phrase as the correct response is likely to be a paraphrase of part of the text.

Exercise 3: Identifying key words in the question

a) Remind students of the activities they did in **Listening** and **Speaking** to help them understand what they were listening for or going to speak about. Point out that it is similar when reading, i.e. if they are clear what information they need to find, it is much easier to identify it in the text. Draw their attention to the Exam tip.

b) Students underline the question words and key words in the five questions. Then elicit the kind of information they will be listening for in each question.

Suggested answers
1 <u>Why</u> are <u>Ben</u>, <u>Rory</u> and <u>Carlos</u> <u>mentioned</u> in the article?
2 <u>Which</u> of the following <u>best describes</u> <u>Ben</u>?
3 <u>What</u> do we <u>know</u> about the <u>lake</u> that <u>Rory visits</u>?
4 <u>Carlos</u> <u>mentions</u> that he is <u>left-handed</u> because …
5 The answers to the <u>recent research</u> and the <u>answers</u> from the <u>readers</u> …

Exercise 4: Answering multiple-choice questions

a) Ask students to re-read the text and do the exercise. They can then compare their answers in groups of five.

b) Once they have determined the correct answers, ask each member in the group to choose one of the questions and explain why all of the other responses are incorrect. Then refer students to the explanations in the answer key.

c) Discuss whether Exercise 3 helped them identify the correct answers.

Typical mistakes: Students who habitually read texts intensively from the first word to the last may be reluctant to read selectively from the text in order to answer the questions. Remind them to use the key words they have underlined to skip to the relevant sections. This will save them time.

Students who answer the questions incorrectly often do so because they rely on their general knowledge or opinion. Explain that for each correct answer they should be able to underline a part of the text that means the same thing.

Answers
1 b   **2** d   **3** b   **4** b   **5** c

Practice for the test (20–30 mins)

This can be done in class as pairwork or assigned for homework. Remind students to look back at the Exam tips in the unit. Point out that students can do more activities online if they want extra practice or to consolidate what they have learnt.

Answers
1 a   2 d   3 a   4 c   5 d   6 d

Writing: Trends and statistics

Student preparation for this class: Have students complete the Online / Workbook language preparation exercises at home before the lesson begins.

Teacher preparation: For Spot check 1, prepare cards with hobbies listed in Exercise 2 of the Workbook or Online (one word per card). Prepare one set of cards for each group of three students. (20–30 mins)

Online / Workbook language preparation

Focus: The purpose of these exercises is to introduce common words and collocations for hobbies and interests; introduce the present simple tense; introduce quantifiers.

Develop your exam skills (Student's Book p. 24)

Focus: These exercises train students to read and correctly interpret tables. Exercises 3 and 4 show how to write a Task 1 introduction based on a table.

Introduction

Use the Spot checks to clarify students' understanding of the Online / Workbook language preparation.

Spot check 1

To reinforce verb-noun collocations for hobbies and interests, write these questions on the board:

- *Do you play football?*
- *How often do you play football?*
- *Do you like playing football?*

Nominate individuals in the class to ask and answer the questions. Check for correct use of the auxiliary verb in responses *Yes, I do* and *No, I don't*, and for the use of expressions *never, every day, once a week,* etc. Then put students in groups of three and do the following activity.

1. Ask or designate one person in each group to act as facilitator using the answer key for Exercise 2 in the Workbook (or Online).

2. Place face down in front of each remaining pair of students one set of cards with hobbies from Exercise 2.

3. Players take it in turn to select the top card and ask each other one of the three questions above using the term on the card.

4. The facilitator allocates one point for each correct question and each correct response.

Spot check 2

To provide further practice in using quantifiers, explain that you are going to conduct a quick class survey.

1. Write 5–6 sentences on the board using *… people in the class like + -ing* and the hobbies listed in the Workbook or Online. Leave a blank space at the start of each sentence for a quantifier: _____ *people in the class like playing football.*

2. Ask students to predict the class's responses by completing each sentence with a quantifier listed in Exercise 4 of the Workbook and Online: *all, a lot of, some, few, not many, not much, no,* e.g. *Not many people in the class play football.*

3. To check their predictions, frame each statement as a question and ask for a show of hands in response, e.g. *Who likes playing football?* See who has made the most accurate predictions.

Exercise 1: Understanding information in a table

a) Spend 2–3 minutes discussing the Exam information. Ask questions, e.g.

Do you have experience of this type of task?

How long does it normally take you to write 150 words in English?

Can you recognize the difference between formal, semi-formal and informal writing?

b) Ask students to do the exercise following the instructions in the book and compare their answers in pairs.

c) Follow up by asking students to compare sentences 2 and 3 and identify which is less formal and why. (Answer: 3, because it contains the contraction *don't*). Invite them to rephrase the sentence to make it more formal. (Answer: *Teenagers do not spend much time swimming*).

> **Typical mistakes:** Some students may believe that *few* is the same as *a few*. Explain that *few = not many* and that *a few = some* (i.e. it is affirmative).

Answers
1 F   2 T   3 T   4 F

Exercise 2: Understanding the type of information a table contains

a) Highlight the Exam tip and then give students time to look at the table in pairs. While they work, go round offering any help they need.

b) Students do the exercise individually and check their answers in pairs. Explain that for Task 1 they will always have to give reasons for any general statements they make about the table or diagram.

Answers

b best explains the table because it includes all the information and uses different words.
a does not include enough information.
c repeats the words in the title so it is not as good as (b).

Exercise 3: Assessing table summaries

a) Draw students' attention to the Exam tip. Tell them to make use of what they have learnt to do the exercise.

b) Discuss as a class why one introduction is better.

> **Typical mistakes:** Students often confuse quantity with percentage. Sentences describing the elements of a table are also challenging to write because of the number of prepositional phrases required. Follow up by rewriting sentence (c) from Exercise 2 on the board with the words in random order and ask students to work in pairs to reconstruct the sentence.

Answers

1 See the circled verbs in the introductions in the right-hand column. The verbs are all in the present simple tense.
2 A's first sentence explains the title of the table accurately. B's first sentence is inaccurate.
3 See the underlined details in the introductions below.
4 Introduction A is better because it explains the table correctly and contains general information. Introduction B does not explain the table correctly and contains too many details.

Introduction A: The table shows how much time the age groups spend on different types of Internet activity. There are six age ranges in the table from 10–15 to over 50. The Internet activities include shopping, browsing, social networking and playing games.

Introduction B: The table shows how much people like the Internet depending on their age. 70% of children between ages 10–15 play games on the Internet, and no children between ages 10–15 like shopping. Most older people browse news sites. They spend 54% of their time reading the news on the Internet.

Exercise 4: Completing a summary

a) Draw students' attention to the Exam tip. Have a student explain why the present tense is usually used: because it talks about what we can see in the table.

b) Have students do the exercise in small groups.

Answers

1 younger age groups   **2** much   **3** 16–20   **4** 10–15
5 No   **6** older   **7** like   **8** shopping

Extension activity (50 mins)

Conduct a class survey of Internet use and create a table to serve as a writing prompt.

1. Ask students to identify how much time they spend (in hours or minutes) each day on average on each of the Internet activities listed in Exercise 2.

2. Put students in groups of 5–6 and designate each group with a letter of the alphabet. Ask the members of each group to share their answers among themselves and derive a total for each activity for the group.

3. Sketch a table on the board like the table in Exercise 2 but replace the age groups with Group A, B, C and so on. Compile the information in the table by asking a spokesperson for each group to report their totals for each activity.

4. Give students 20 minutes to write up their findings following the model in Exercise 4.

Practice for the test (40 mins)

This can be done in class or assigned for homework. If this is students' first attempt at Task 1, suggest they spend up to 40 minutes on the task. This is to allow them to develop the skills they need to produce good quality work. As they become more proficient, the amount of time they spend on practice exam tasks can be gradually reduced until they can complete the work within the time allotted in the actual exam. Point out that students can do more activities online if they want extra practice or to consolidate what they have learnt.

Model answer

The table shows the number of people in millions who watch sports on television. It shows the number of viewers for four sports in four different countries.

The table shows that more Americans watch sport on television than the other three nationalities. In all four countries tennis is the most popular sport on television. The total number of viewers for tennis is nearly 26 million, and in each country about 6–7 million people watch it.

Not many people like watching motor racing on television compared to the other sports. In the USA and Canada only 1–1.5 million people watch motor racing but it is more popular in the UK and Australia. Golf is very popular in the USA with 11 million viewers but it is not as popular in the other countries.

UNIT 3: DIFFERENT CULTURES

Speaking: Celebrations

Student preparation for this class: Have students complete the Online / Workbook language preparation exercises at home before the lesson begins.

Teacher preparation: None

Online / Workbook language preparation

Focus: These exercises introduce language for talking about special occasions: introducing words associated with festivities; introducing connecting words; the past simple tense; pronunciation of past simple verbs and -ed.

Develop your exam skills (Student's Book p. 26)

Focus: These exercises focus on Part 3 of the Speaking test: Two-way discussion: Exercises 1–4 focus on understanding the examiner's questions; Exercises 5–6 train students to give relevant answers of an appropriate length; Exercises 6–7 provide an opportunity to practise.

Introduction

1   Introduce the unit by getting students to talk about the pictures on pages 28 and 32 in pairs. Ask them to talk about what they can see and how it relates to the unit topic, *Different cultures* and the Speaking section, *Celebrations*. Elicit information from students and have them guess what the other sections will be about. (The Korean marriage ceremony relates to celebrations; the others could be about British culture and about how people live in different countries.)

2   Use one of the Spot checks to clarify students' understanding of the Online / Workbook language preparation. You can use the other Spot check at an appropriate time during the lesson.

Spot check 1

To check students' recall of vocabulary associated with special occasions do the following activity.

1.   On the board, write the verbs *celebrate, give, make, visit, watch, wear,* and the nouns *family, presents, costumes, traditional food, New Year, fireworks.*

2.   Have students work in groups of three to write six sentences, each containing one of the verbs and one of the nouns on the board. See which group can make the most correct sentences in the shortest time.

Spot check 2

To provide practice using the past simple tense, play noughts and crosses using irregular verbs from the unit.

---

1.   On the board in a 3 x 3 grid, write the verbs *be, eat, get, go, have, meet, see, sing* and *wear.*

2.   Put students in two teams: 'noughts' (0) and 'crosses' (X).

3.   Teams take turns to select a word and use it in a sentence in the past simple tense.

4.   If a team uses the word correctly, they win the square. (Whilst adjudicating, focus on correct use of the verb and ignore other errors that do not significantly impede comprehension.)

5.   The team that is able to win three consecutive squares (horizontally, vertically or diagonally) wins the game.

Exercise 1: Understanding a Part 2 task card

a)   Go over the Exam information on timing in the Speaking test and how Part 3 works. Spend a few minutes discussing how students feel about this part of the exam. Then do the exercises together as a class.

b)   Have students match the topics to the three task cards.

c)   Students feed back on which topic they would prefer to talk about and why.

Answers
a 3   **b** 2   **c** 1

Exercise 2: Understanding Part 3 questions

a)   Highlight the Exam tip and how the topics in Part 2, which students have just discussed, will prepare them for Part 3.

b)   Students match questions a–c to the task cards in Exercise 1.

Answers
a 3   **b** 2   **c** 1

 ### Exercise 3: Understanding key words in questions

Students do the exercises following the instructions in the book and compare their answers in pairs.

Answers
1 Is it <u>important</u> for <u>a country</u> to have <u>festivals</u>?
2 Are <u>friends</u> <u>more important</u> than <u>family</u>?

Exercise 4: Matching a question and answer

a)   Students read the two answers and match them to the question in Exercise 3.

b)   Elicit in what way the two answers are different, but don't go into any detail at this stage.

Typical mistakes: Students may have difficulty hearing unstressed words such as *an* and *of*. Point out that in most cases, hearing the words that are stressed will give them a good enough understanding of the question.

Answer
1 Is it important for a country to have festivals?

Exercise 5: Evaluating answers

a) Have students work in pairs, with one student evaluating response A and the other evaluating response B.

b) Pairs share their answers. Then discuss as a class.

Answers
1 A Yes   B Yes
2 A Yes. The speaker also extends the answer to include other countries.
B No. The speaker talks about a personal experience of a festival, not about the importance of a country having festivals.
3 A Yes: *In my country*, we … It is *important*. … I like travelling to *other countries* …
B Yes: *I went to a festival* … *It was* important to me because …
4 A Yes (seven sentences)   B No (two sentences)

Exercise 6: Using link words

Students discuss the answer in pairs. During feedback explain that link words can help students keep talking while they think of how to continue and also signal to the examiner how they will continue.

also: giving additional information

I think: giving an opinion

I mean: providing clarification

In addition, each link word or phrase keeps the flow of the answer.

Exercise 7: Asking and answering a Part 3 question

a) Give students 5–10 minutes to prepare their answers. Refer them to the Grammar section: *Verbs for talking about the past.*

b) Have students ask and answer in pairs.

c) If possible, students then record their answers and assess them using the questions in Exercise 5.

> **Typical mistakes:** Some students may give short answers in order to avoid the risk of making mistakes. Point out that the examiner will focus more on what they can do with English than on the mistakes that they make.

Extension activity (20 mins)

To provide further practice in answering Speaking Part 3 questions, do the following activity.

1. Elicit as many questions based on the stem as you can.

2. Ask each student in the class to choose one of the questions.

3. Have students stand up and circulate, asking each other their questions. Instruct them to change partners after every minute.

 # Practice for the test (20–30 mins)

This can be done in class as pairwork or assigned for homework. Remind students to look back at the Exam tips in the unit. Point out that students can do more activities online if they want extra practice or to consolidate what they have learnt.

Part 2
Answers
Exercise 1
Model answer
special occasion: graduation
where: university, England
when: last summer
who: my family
explain how you felt: excited, nervous

Exercise 2
Model answer
My special occasion was my graduation ceremony. There was a parade with the professors and the other students. Then we went into a hall for the ceremony and we got our certificates. I graduated in England from Oxford University. It was last summer. It was very hot. My family flew to England for the ceremony and we celebrated together. I was very excited because my family came to visit me. I was nervous too. It was a very important day.

Part 3
Exercise 4
Model answers
What is an important festival in your country?
An important festival in my country is New Year's Eve. There is a big parade and a carnival. Tourists visit the city and watch the festival. It is a special evening.

What are your favourite parts of this festival?
My favourite parts of the festival are the music and the clothes. I enjoy watching the parade and the beautiful costumes. I really like singing and dancing to the music. It's fun.

How have special occasions such as weddings changed in your country?
I think that weddings are the same. In my country we are proud of our traditions. The family go to a special building for the wedding ceremony. Then there are two or three meals for other family and friends.

Reading: British culture

Student preparation for this class: Have students complete the Online / Workbook vocabulary preparation exercises at home before the lesson begins.

Teacher preparation: None.

Online / Workbook vocabulary preparation

Focus: The purpose of these activities is to review and extend vocabulary for places, games and food in Britain, and check understanding of words for different regions in the United Kingdom.

Develop your exam skills (Student's Book p. 28)

Focus: These exercises train students to understand text organization and help them to match headings to sections of text.

Introduction

Use one of the Spot checks to clarify students' understanding of the Online / Workbook vocabulary preparation. You can use the other Spot check at an appropriate time during the lesson.

Spot check 1

To check students' recall of names for places, objects, food and drink in England, write the following words from the Online / Workbook Exercises 1, 3 and 4 on the board: *City Hall, the Old Bailey, the Gherkin, the Palace of Westminster, tearoom, kettle, teapot, Cornish pasty, smoothie, duck-duck-goose, scones, haggis, elderflower cordial, rarebit, leek.*

1. Ask students to tell you which word(s) go with the definitions you say to them, e.g. *It's a place that looks like a vegetable* (the Gherkin). *It's something you use to boil water* (a kettle).

2. Ask students to write two definitions for words they pick themselves.

3. Put students in groups of three or four. They then take it in turns to read out their definitions; the other group members listen to the definitions and guess the words.

4. You can make the game harder by removing the words from the board after students have finished writing their definitions. Give them time to have another look before you do so.

Spot check 2

To review vocabulary for places, objects, food and drink in England, have a class quiz.

1. Put students in two or more teams. Explain that you are going to have a quiz about England and that each team must write four questions to ask the other team(s).

2. Remind them to refer to the information in their Workbooks or Online when writing their questions. Write some question prompts on the board to help with ideas:

    What is (the Gherkin)?

    What happens in (the Palace of Westminster)?

    What sort of food is (England) famous for?

    How do you make (tea) in England?

3. When the teams have written their questions, they take it in turns to put them to the other team(s).

 Exercise 1: Identifying what a text is about

a) Go over the Exam information on matching headings. Remind students that they have already looked at the techniques of skimming and scanning in Unit 2. Explain that Exercise 1 will help them understand what the text on page 28 is about.

b) Have students read paragraph A individually following the instructions in the book. Discuss their answers, emphasizing that answers may vary. Challenge them to explain why they underlined the sections that they did.

Answer
1 It is not easy to compare the artistic styles and periods of different countries. This is partly ...

Exercise 2: Identifying links to the main paragraph

a) Have students read paragraph B and identify links to the main paragraph as a class. Accept any answer and discuss why it is relevant or why not. If necessary, write the following headings on the board. You can then elicit words from the text (shown below in italics) that relate to these headings.

    Artistic styles: *Victorian*
    Periods: *the twentieth century*
    Different countries: *confusion / non-British people / who know little about it*
    Different words for same features: *different styles can be called Victorian*
    Styles and periods overlap: *Queen Victoria's reign lasted from 1837 until her death in 1901. Secondly, the Victorian style itself continued right into the twentieth century ...*

b) Have students read paragraphs C and D and underline any other links to the main paragraph.

Suggested answers
B An example of this is the 'Victorian' period ... British royal history, which could create confusion to non-British people who know little about it – Queen Victoria's reign lasted from 1837 until her death in 1901, Secondly, the Victorian style itself continued right into the twentieth century, and it could be argued that there are different styles that can be called Victorian ...
C Despite Victorian times being characterized by romanticism, the famous British romantic poets belong to the period before Queen Victoria. ... And, even if we know they can all be described as Georgian artists, which King George does this refer to? Actually, it refers to four of them (George I, George II, George III and George IV), covering a long period including most of the eighteenth century and some of the nineteenth. But then again, there was a Georgian revival in the twentieth century. Moreover, the style itself incorporates previous styles, including gothic; it also has its own subdivision ...
D The period after the Victorian era is referred to as Edwardian, after Edward VII ... Unsurprisingly, nobody is sure whether 1910 is the correct end point for the period. ... And then, in other European countries, the Art Nouveau era ended around the same time ...

Exercise 3: Using signposting language

a) Point out that certain words and phrases, such as the ones in Exercise 3, can help the reader follow a text. Go over the example and clarify the concept of 'signposting'.

b) Ask students to do the exercise following the instructions in the book and compare their answers in pairs. Feed back as a class. Refer to the Grammar section: *Adverbs that introduce further explanation*.

Answers
first of all (B): introduces the first reason why it is difficult to describe 'Victorian'
secondly (B): gives the next reason for the difficulty
despite (C): introduces a contrast
then again (C): introduces another complicating factor
moreover (C): introduces another reason why it is difficult to say what 'Georgian' refers to
unsurprisingly (D): indicates that by now the reader will not be surprised at what he/she reads

Exercise 4: Identifying organization of a text

a) Point out that students will have already identified particular periods in Exercise 2. Tell them to circle each period and think about how each one clarifies the general theme.

b) Follow up by explaining any problems that students have with the concepts of *Victorian*, *Edwardian* and *Georgian* times.

Answers
B Victorian   **C** Georgian (also mentioned: Georgian revival, gothic, Regency)   **D** Edwardian (and Art Nouveau)

Exercise 5: Concluding an essay
Ask students to do the exercise following the instructions in the book and compare their answers in groups. Feed back as a class.

> **Typical mistakes:** Students may not have thought carefully about the role of the conclusion in a text and this may mean that they find it hard to identify key features or write effective conclusions to their own essays. Go over the function of the conclusion: draw their attention to examples of effective conclusions and spend some time discussing what makes an effective conclusion.

Answer
Point **a** is <u>essential</u>: the conclusion should pick up the main point.
Point **b** is important as referring back to the main ideas brings the text together.
Points **c** and **e** <u>emphasize the relevance</u> of the text as they link the issue that is explained in the text to real-life consequences.
Point **d** is <u>unsuitable</u>: conclusions should not include new information.

Extension activity (25 mins)
To raise awareness of the type of exam question that involves choosing headings, ask students to look at another text (e.g. the one on page 12) and decide on a heading for each paragraph.

Have them work in groups to compare their headings and choose the one they like best.

Practice for the test (30 mins)

This can be done in class as pairwork or assigned for homework. Remind students to look back at the Exam tips in the unit. Point out that students can do more activities online if they want extra practice or to consolidate what they have learnt.

Answers
Section A: 2   Section B: 10   Section C: 3   Section D: 5
Section E: 1   Section F: 7

Listening: Comparing lifestyles

> **Student preparation for this class:** Have students complete the Online / Workbook vocabulary preparation exercises at home before the lesson begins.
>
> **Teacher preparation:** None

Online / Workbook vocabulary preparation

> **Focus:** The purpose of these activities is to introduce vocabulary related to culture, food, dress and housing; the difference between *make*, *have* and *do*.

Develop your exam skills (Student's Book p. 31)

> **Focus:** Exercises 1–2 focus on language used for comparing and contrasting; Exercises 3–5 train students to answer multiple-choice matching information questions in the Listening test on the subject of food and weddings.

Introduction
Use the Spot checks to clarify students' understanding of the Online / Workbook vocabulary preparation.

> **Spot check**
>
> To reinforce the vocabulary related to culture, do a word sorting exercise.
>
> 1. Get students to close their books.
>
> 2. Write all the words from the word map in Exercise 2 from the Workbook or Online on the board in random order: *alphabet, block of flats, brick, concrete, cotton, culture, diet, hat, headdress, house, national costume, material, pronunciation, scarf, silk, spicy, sweet, taste* and *vegetarian*.
>
>   Circle the four words that are the main headings: *Communication, Diet, National costume* and *Housing*.
>
> 3. Put students in groups of three and have them write the words under the four main headings.

4. Have a class discussion to check the grouping of the words and answer questions about any of the words.

Exercise 1: Identifying words for comparing and contrasting

a) Books closed, write these sentences on the board:

Compare your language with English and contrast your language with English.

Ask students what they think the difference is. After discussion, point out that *compare* means 'to look at things to see how they are similar and how they are different', whereas *contrast* means 'to look at things to see how they are different'.

b) Put students in groups of three and ask them to make a list of comparing and contrasting language, e.g. *the same as*, *different from*. After a few minutes, ask students to look at page 31 and the words in Exercise 1.

c) Play the recording (track 23) and have them underline the words they hear. Ask students to compare their answers with each other.

Answers
the same as   more [common] than   much more [open]
in comparison with   [friendlier] than

Exercise 2: Completing tables

a) The table in Exercise 2 is a good way of practising adverbs that emphasize similarity or limit similarity. Point out that these words can all go in front of the adjective *similar*, as in the phrase *extremely similar*. Refer to the Grammar section: *Modifying adverbs used with comparisons.*

b) Ask students to do the exercise individually and then check their answers in pairs. Have students study the sentences under the table carefully.

Answers

To emphasize similarity	To limit similarity
very	a bit
extremely	rather
incredibly	quite
exactly	not
	a little

 ## Exercise 3: Listening for relevant information

a) Draw students' attention to the Exam information. Make sure they understand that in this question type they will not hear the speakers in the same order as on the question sheet.

b) Before students listen to the recording, have them read the question and try to guess the answers. This prediction is an important step in preparing to listen. Then play the recording (track 24) and have them find the answers.

Answers
1 b   2 c   3 e

Exercise 4: Turning sentence stems into questions

a) Draw students' attention to the Exam tip. Point out the technique of changing a sentence stem into a question.

b) Students then work individually and turn the sentence stems into questions. Have them compare their answers in pairs.

Answers
1 In traditional Indian families, where did the bride and groom meet for the first time?
2 In India, what did the father of the bride use to do?
3 What has it become popular for Indian families to do recently?
4 Where does the couple live after they are married?

 ## Exercise 5: Answering multiple-choice questions

a) Have students read the questions carefully and predict their answers. Then ask them to work in pairs to compare what they think the answers to the questions might be.

b) Play the recording (track 25) and have students compare their answers.

Answers
1 b   2 c   3 a   4 b

Extension activity (20 mins)

To provide further practice in listening to comparisons and contrasts, have students take it in turns to give a talk on two people they know well (e.g. family members).

1. Tell students they are going to prepare and then give a talk comparing and contrasting two people they know well. Give an example of things they can say, e.g. *My father likes watching football, but my mother likes watching movies*.

2. Give students 10 minutes to prepare and make notes while you monitor and help with language.

3. Put students in groups of four and let them take it in turns to give their talk to the rest of the group using the language introduced in the unit.

 ## Practice for the test (30 mins)

This can be done in class as pairwork or assigned for homework. Remind students to look back at the Exam tips in the unit. Point out that students can do more activities online if they want extra practice or to consolidate what they have learnt.

Answers
1 b   2 b   3 a   4 c   5 g   6 water festivals   7 six   8 life, wealth, luck   9 New Year   10 (by) ancient tradition

Writing: World culture

Student preparation for this class: Have students complete the Online / Workbook language preparation exercises at home before the lesson begins.

Teacher preparation: Download and print out the Spot check handout (one per student). For the Extension activity, prepare bundles of 10–12 blank slips of paper (one set for each group of four students). (30 mins)

Online / Workbook language preparation

Focus: The purpose of these activities is to introduce common nouns associated with culture and a range of negative and positive adjectives; introduce *Subject + Verb + Object* word order and common conjunctions.

Develop your exam skills (Student's Book p. 34)

Focus: Exercises 1–5 focus on understanding Task 2 essay questions. Exercise 6 focuses on generating ideas for a Task 2 essay.

Introduction

Use one of the Spot checks to clarify students' understanding of the Online / Workbook language preparation. You can use the other Spot check at an appropriate time during the lesson.

> **Spot check**
>
> To check students' recall of adjectives, put students in groups of 3–4. Distribute the Spot check 1 handout and invite students to respond to what they see using the adjectives listed in Exercise 2 of the Workbook: *useful, dangerous, interesting, tiring, creative, amazing, beautiful, harmless, terrible.*

Exercise 1: Matching essay title to topic

a) Spend 3–4 minutes discussing the Exam information. Check understanding by asking questions, e.g.

Have you written essays of this type before, either in English or in your own language?

How long does it normally take you to write 250 words in English?

How do you learn about the kind of social topics covered in Task 2 exam questions?

b) Ask students to do the exercise following the instructions in the book and compare their answers in small groups.

> **Typical mistakes:** Students who choose (a) or (b) for question 1, or choose an incorrect paraphrase for the question, may focus too much on the subordinate clause (*because they are …*). Point out that in most cases the important information in a statement is contained in the main clause (*All museums and art galleries should be free …*).

Answer
c free entrance to museums and art galleries

Exercise 2: Matching question to essay title

Students do the exercise individually and check their answers in pairs or small groups.

> **Typical mistakes:** If students choose (a), point out that IELTS Task 2 questions are rarely so broad. For those who choose (c), point out that essay questions are unlikely to be so categorical or 'black and white'.

Answer
b How far do you agree that it is a good idea for museums and art galleries to be free for cultural reasons?

Exercise 3: Understanding cause and effect

a) Highlight the Exam tip. Point out that the exam question in Exercise 3 includes two opinions, a cause and an effect. Elicit what they are.

b) Students work in pairs and follow the instructions.

Answer
a To what extent do you agree that if children watch too much television, they do not learn or develop well?

Exercise 4: Identifying matching opinions

a) Students work in pairs to complete the exercise. Refer to the Grammar section: *Expressing ideas and opinions.*

b) Conduct a straw poll of students' opinions regarding statements 1–4: as you read out each statement, ask for a show of hands if they agree.

c) Follow up by having pairs generate 2–3 ideas of their own in response to the essay question. Invite each pair to read out one of their ideas and ask the class to decide whether they agree or disagree with the statement in the essay question.

Answers
1 D 2 A 3 A 4 D

Exercise 5: Understanding the questions

a) Draw students' attention to the Exam tip. Point out that students lose marks if they write about topics in general rather than the specific question.

b) Discuss the example. Then have students do the exercise individually and check their answers in pairs.

Answers
2 Q 3 Q 4 T 5 Q 6 Q

Exercise 6: Generating ideas for writing

a) Highlight the Exam tip. Emphasize the importance of spending some time thinking before beginning to write. Refer to the Grammar section: *Linking words for connecting ideas.*

b) Students complete the sentences and feed back as a class.

c) Have students brainstorm more ideas in small groups. Invite a spokesperson from each group to share one or two of their ideas with the class. As they do so, write them up on the board in note form.

d) Students add four or five of their own ideas to the list.

Suggested answers

1 Traditional culture is important *because it helps to keep a country's identity alive*.

2 Modern culture is important because it *helps us understand the world today*.

3 Young people often prefer modern culture but *it is not always better than traditional culture*.

4 Both traditional and modern culture are popular so *we should encourage both of them*.

Extension activity (25 mins)

Students continue working in small groups. Distribute 10–12 slips of blank paper to each group and ask them to write down one of the ideas generated in Exercise 5 on each slip of paper. Ask them to put the ideas in the order in which they might logically occur in an essay. Circulate among the groups and ask them to explain their choices.

Practice for the test (60 mins)

This can be assigned for homework. Suggest that students spend up to 60 minutes on the exercise. This is to allow them to develop the skills they need to produce good quality work. As students become more proficient, the amount of time they spend on practice exam tasks can be gradually reduced until they can complete the work within the time allotted in the exam. Point out that students can do more activities online if they want extra practice or to consolidate what they have learnt.

Task 2

Model answer

Some people think that young people should spend their free time on cultural activities like music, film and theatre. Others believe that playing sport is better for young people. In my opinion, both cultural activities and sports are important parts of life so young people should do a mixture of both.

Sport gives young people the chance to exercise, which is important for health reasons. Sport also teaches young people about rules and teamwork. Cultural activities are good for the health of the mind and spirit and allow young people to be creative and experience different worlds. However, going to the theatre or learning a musical instrument can be expensive. Sports activities can be less expensive but can be dangerous and lead to injury.

In my opinion, doing only one type of activity – just sport or just music, for example – can be bad. Many young people concentrate on one activity in order to become the best, like young sports stars. This can put a lot of pressure on them and make them less interesting than someone who does a variety of things.

I believe that young people should have the chance to do a variety of activities and that a balance of sport and cultural activities is best.

UNIT 4: PLACES TO LIVE

Speaking: Different cities

Student preparation for this class: Have students complete the Online / Workbook language preparation exercises at home before the lesson begins.

Teacher preparation: None

Online / Workbook language preparation

Focus: The purpose of these exercises is to introduce words for places and activities in cities; introduce phrases to describe cities; focus on syllables and word stress; focus on the difference between *There is* and *There are*; revision.

Develop your exam skills (Student's Book p. 36)

Focus: These exercises focus on Parts 1 and 2 of the Speaking test. Exercises 1–6 train students to talk about everyday topics and to give longer answers at a natural speed; Exercises 7–8 practise planning and organizing ideas when talking about a specific topic.

Introduction

1   Introduce the unit by getting students to talk about the pictures on pages 38 and 39 in pairs. Ask them to talk about what they can see and how it might relate to the unit topic, *Places to live* and the Speaking section, *Different cities*. Elicit information from students and have them guess what the other sections will be about (e.g. the photo of London could represent cities; the halls of residence, living on campus; the basketball court, amenities; the volunteers planting trees, communities).

2   Use one of the Spot checks to clarify students' understanding of the Online / Workbook language preparation. You can use the other Spot check at an appropriate time during the lesson.

Spot check 1

To check the students' recall of names for places and activities in cities, write the words for places from Exercises 1 and 3 in the Workbook or Online: *football stadium, gallery, harbour, market, museum, shopping mall, beach, bridge, café, factory, gallery, hotel, park, river, skyscraper, theatre*.

1.   Ask students to tell you which words go with the sentences you say to them, e.g. *You can buy clothes here* (possible answer: *shopping mall*). *You can swim here* (possible answers: *river, beach*).

2.   Once students have become confident with this, ask them to choose two words themselves and write two sentences for them.

3.   Put students in groups of 3–4. The group members listen to the sentences and guess the words. You can make the game harder by

removing the words from the board after students have finished writing their own sentences. Give them time to have another look before you do so.

Spot check 2

To check the students' recall of words to describe cities, put the following grid on the board:

The people are …	It has …	It is near …	It is famous for …

1.   As a group, students fill in the grid for the city or town where you are.

2.   Then have students work in pairs to describe a place that they have visited, e.g. on holiday.

Exercise 1: Assessing a written answer to Part 1

a)   Have students read the Exam tip before doing the exercise. Then ask them to read Exercise 1, make notes individually and compare their answers in pairs.

b)   Discuss the good and bad points of the answer with the class and explain that Exercises 2–6 will give them a chance to improve it.

Answers
Good: The grammar is correct and the vocabulary is appropriate for the topic.
Bad: The answer is too short for Part 1.

Exercise 2: Preparing and practising a Part 1 answer

a)   Students work individually on making notes.

b)   Students ask and answer the question in pairs. Then ask them to mingle with other students in the class to ask and answer the question.

Possible answers
• near the border, population 100,000
• clean, exciting, friendly
• museums, theatres
• very friendly, people always kind

Exercise 3: Recording a Part 1 answer

If possible, students record their answers using their mobile phones.

Exercise 4: Assessing answers

a)   Play the recording (track 29). Have students work in pairs and assess the answer using the table.

b)   Students then assess each other's recording using the same form.

Answers
The answer is too fast. There are some pauses. There are no grammar errors. Some words are repeated, e.g. *capital city, I like, people*.

Exercise 5: Improving answers

a) Organize the students in different pairs to help each other improve their answers.

b) They then record their answers and discuss the improvements.

> **Typical mistakes:** Students tend to speak unnaturally slowly. Once they have practised and have gained confidence, they will speak more naturally. However, you need to monitor their performance to make sure that they speak clearly and at a natural pace.

Exercise 6: Assessing and improving Part 2 notes

a) Draw students' attention to the Exam tip. With books closed, have them answer questions about what they have just read, e.g. *How long should you speak for? How many topics do you need to speak about? How fast should you speak? How long do you have to think and plan?*

b) Have students discuss the notes in Exercise 6 in groups of three. Feed back as a class.

Answers
• description of country
• other cities I like

The topic card does not ask for this information and talking about it will waste time.

Exercise 7: Preparing notes for a Part 2 question

Make sure students know what to do. Refer to the Grammar section: *Adjectives*. Then give them one minute to prepare their notes. Be strict about time and they will improve through practice.

Exercise 8: Improving a Part 2 answer

a) Give students an opportunity to improve their notes. Point out that they will not have this time in the exam.

b) Tell students you will time them recording their answer. Give them two minutes. You will probably find that many students finish early. If so, discuss with the class how they can learn to speak for the full two minutes. Give them another opportunity to record their answers.

> **Typical mistakes:** Students often tend to write sentences rather than notes. If they do this, draw their attention to the short notes in Exercise 6. Point out that there are useful headings (e.g. *tourists – try food, take photos*), grammatical notes (*there's ...*), and vocabulary notes (*relax, meet friends, play sports*).

 Extension activity (30 mins)
To raise awareness of the content of Part 2 questions, ask students to study the topic cards in Exercise 6 and **Practice for the test**. Elicit the similarities and differences. Ask them to write a similar question and then work in pairs to ask and answer each other's questions.

Practice for the test (20–30 mins)

This can be done in class as pairwork or assigned for homework. Remind students to look back at the Exam tips in the unit. Point out that students can do more activities online if they want extra practice or to consolidate what they have learnt.

Answers
Part 1
Exercise 1
1 a **2** d **3** b **4** f **5** c **6** g **7** e

Part 2
Exercise 4
Model answer
Yes, last week I went to Dubai and I was there because I was visiting my best friend. So what I really like about Dubai was the fact that I was there visiting my friend and it was a great place. It's not so far from my country, first of all, and it is in the UAE. It is near Abu Dhabi and I flew to the airport there. My friend, he met me, and we drove to Dubai. It was maybe one hour until the outskirts, then the traffic was very bad. In Dubai, you have to take the car everywhere. We relaxed and went to the shopping malls, they are great, and the beaches. We chatted mainly. We hadn't seen each other for a long time. And we went skiing! In the shopping mall there is a slope. It was interesting because it has many contrasts, because you have lots of poor people and lots of very, very rich people. There is no middle class there and the places you go, there is gold, too much gold and on the other hand, there are many people living there, they are immigrants.

Writing: Living in cities

> **Student preparation for this class:** Have students complete the Online / Workbook language preparation exercises at home before the lesson begins.

> **Teacher preparation:** For Spot check 1, download, copy and cut up resource material (one set per group of six students). (15 mins)

Online / Workbook language preparation

> **Focus:** The purpose of these exercises is to introduce words describing urban areas and buildings, and verbs associated with changes to them; introduce the present perfect for recent changes that are either still continuing or relevant to the present; introduce comparative and superlative forms.

Develop your exam skills (Student's Book p. 38)

> **Focus:** These exercises train students to describe two or more charts, graphs or tables in preparation for writing one of the question types in Task 1.

Introduction

Use one of the Spot checks to clarify students' understanding of the Online / Workbook language preparation. You can use the other Spot check at an appropriate time during the lesson.

Spot check 1

To check students' recall of words associated with urban change, have them play a game in groups of six.

1. Hand out one of the building / urban areas cards to each student in a group and place the set of verb cards face down in the middle of the group.

2. Students take it in turns to pick up a verb card and make a sentence with their building / urban area, e.g. *deteriorate / industrial complex*: *The industrial complex in my town is deteriorating.*

3. The other students in the group judge whether the sentence is grammatically correct and makes sense. If so, the student keeps the card. If not, they replace it at the bottom of the pile. The winner is the student who has the most cards at the end of the game. Note that sentences should have some real content, so *The industrial complex in my town is deteriorating* is acceptable, but *The industrial complex is deteriorating* is not.

Spot check 2

To provide practice in using the present perfect, have students write one sentence about something unusual they have done in their life (using the present perfect). They hand in their sentences for you to read out one by one to the class. Students write down who they think has done each unusual thing. The winner is the person who makes the most correct guesses.

Exercise 1: Completing information about a bar chart

a) Remind students that they have already done some work on trends and statistics in table form in Unit 2. In this unit they will compare information in the form of tables, bar charts, pie charts and graphs. Spend 2–3 minutes discussing the Exam information. Ask questions, e.g.

   Will you have to compare data about different topics? You read about changes in Summerville in Exercise 4 in the Workbook or Online. Can you name two different aspects relating to houses? How might one change have caused another?

b) Ask students to discuss the bar chart and two pie charts in pairs and make sure they understand the data. This is an opportunity for them to ask you questions. Refer to the Grammar section: *Prepositions for when things happen*.

c) Have them complete Exercise 1 individually and compare their answers in pairs.

Answers
2 2000s and 2010s   **3** lower   **4** cheaper / less expensive
5 cost of renting an apartment   **6** entertainment and food and clothing

Exercise 2: Identifying main trends and details

a) Draw attention to the Exam tip. Point out that the main trends refer to things in general. The first example talks about general activities, i.e. spending on 'other things'. In other cases the general thing could be the time frame.

b) Have students complete the exercise in pairs and check their answers as a group. Point out that this is an introduction to tables and charts and they will do more practice in later units.

Answers
2 M   **3** M   **4** M   **5** D   **6** D   **7** D

Exercise 3: Answering *True / False* questions

a) Students complete the exercise individually and check their answers in pairs or small groups.

b) During feedback have students explain why two sentences use the present perfect and the four others the past simple (sentences 1 and 2 describe periods up to the present; sentences 3–6 describe points or periods in the past).

> **Typical mistakes:** Students at all levels find the present perfect difficult to understand. It is useful to contrast it with the past simple at every opportunity.

Answers
2 F   **3** F   **4** T   **5** F   **6** T

Exercise 4: Expanding notes

a) Draw attention to the Exam tip. Then focus on how the notes for item 1 have been expanded: the time period moved to the beginning of the sentence (but it could remain at the end); addition of two definite articles; equals (=) to indicate a change (in this case using the present perfect); *so* to indicate consequence; noun phrase + two nouns changed to verbs *(land use, increase / decrease)*. Refer to the Grammar section: *Present perfect*.

b) Have students do the exercise individually and check their answers in pairs or small groups.

> **Typical mistakes:** Students often find it difficult to edit their work. Creating full sentences from notes is a very good opportunity for them to focus on accuracy using ready-made chunks of language. Encourage them to make good use of this opportunity and link it to the importance of editing their own work.

Suggested answers
2 From 1990 to 2000 the cost of business land rose only slightly so the land used for shops and offices in Newtown remained the same.
3 Since 2000 the cost of business land and the amount of land used for business have remained stable.
4 The amount of land used for housing in Newtown has decreased over the last 40 years due to the increase in the cost of residential land.
5 The amount of land used for offices in Newtown grew from 1980 to 2000.
6 Between 1980 and 2010 the cheapest type of land in Newtown was park land.

Have students produce a complete summary of the data in the graph and bar chart on page 39 using the 12 sentences in Exercises 3 and 4.

Practice for the test (30 mins)

This can be done in class or assigned for homework. Tell students to spend up to 30 minutes on the exercise at this stage. Point out that students can do more activities online if they want extra practice or to consolidate what they have learnt

Task 1
Model answer
The pie charts and table show 25-year-olds' accommodation and the availability of different types of housing in London in the 1990s and 2010s. Since 2010 the lower number of available 1–2 bedroom houses and flats has reduced the housing choices for this age group.

Shared accommodation has become the most common form of housing for this age group in the 2010s. In the 1990s, only around 50% of those surveyed lived in shared houses or flats. In the 2010s this number has grown to around 75% of 25-year-olds living in London. The higher number could be due to the stable availability of larger houses and flats during this period.

There was also a drop in the number of people living alone. In the 1990s around a quarter of 25-year-olds lived alone in London. However, from 2010 onwards, the reduction in the availability of 1–2 bedroom houses and flats has altered this figure. In the 1990s there were 34,000 1–2 bedroom houses and 32,000 1–2 bedroom flats available. These figures dropped to 12,000 and 10,000 from 2010 onwards.

Finally, living with parents has become less common. There was a reduction in the number of 25-year-olds living with parents from around a third in the 1990s to under a quarter in 2010.

Reading: Creating communities

Student preparation for this class: Have students complete the Online / Workbook vocabulary preparation exercises at home before the lesson begins.

Teacher preparation: For the Extension activity, cut up strips of paper (long enough to write sentences on); prepare three strips for each student. (10 mins)

Online / Workbook vocabulary preparation

Focus: The purpose of these exercises is to introduce words related to groups and types of community; focus on word building and ways of categorizing words; focus on compound nouns connected with groups of people.

Develop your exam skills (Student's Book p. 41)

Focus: These exercises train students to match topics, statements or opinions to particular sections of a text.

Introduction
Use the Spot checks to clarify students' understanding of the Online / Workbook vocabulary preparation.

Spot check
To reinforce vocabulary related to community groups, do the following activity.
1. Put students in teams of four.
2. Give them one minute to write down as many compounds and phrases as they can containing the word *community* (without looking in their books).
3. After one minute see which team has the longest list. Have them read out their list and write the phrases on the board.

Exercise 1: Categorizing vocabulary
a) Have students do the exercise following the instructions in the book.

b) During feedback, ask them to explain why they chose to categorize the words as they did.

Answers

Category 1: meaning (groups)	Category 2: pronouns	Category 3: adjectives
organization	he	educational
community	her	communal
team	they	practical
cast	she	loyal
crowd	theirs	academic
band	them	criminal
party	mine	safe

Exercise 2: Matching features in text
a) Go over the Exam information on matching features. Introduce the newsletter and draw attention to the glossary at the end of the text.

b) Have students think about the example and feed back as a class.

c) Students do the exercise individually and compare their answers in groups. Emphasize that several different answers are possible.

Suggested answers
B new trees
C Oral History / History project / training day
D (events') sponsors / sponsoring
E fountain damage / graffiti damage / minimizing damage
F Forest Schools / Schools activities
G Egg Roll / Easter competition / Egg competition

Exercise 3: Identifying specific topics
a) Remind students of the technique of scanning. Point out that if they know what they are looking for, they can find it more easily. Do the first item as a class and students will find that *money* is mentioned

directly in A, B and G (you might have to point out that it is mentioned indirectly (*sponsors*) in D.

b) Ask students to do the exercise following the instructions in the book and compare their answers in groups.

Answers
1 A, B, D (sponsoring), G   2 D   3 E   4 F, G   5 D, F, G
6 A, D   7 B, C

Exercise 4: Identifying paraphrases in a text

a) Point out that paraphrases are an important part of the IELTS exam as students will have to identify paraphrases in reading texts.

b) Students do the exercise following the instructions in the book. Make sure students underline the paraphrases so you can monitor them as they work.

> **Typical mistakes:** Some students may spend a long time looking through the whole text for paraphrases of specific sentences. Remind them that Exercises 2 and 3 involved skimming to find the topics and scanning for details of specific paragraphs. They should use this information to help them locate the sentences that need paraphrasing, e.g. sentence 3 relates to chocolate eggs, which have already been identified as the topic of paragraph G.

Answers
1 Lots of new trees have gone in recently.
2 The group will be meeting again and will have the opportunity to do some practice interviews.
3 There was a huge response to the Forest Schools activities …
4 All sessions must be booked in advance …
5 The first past the finishing line will win a massive chocolate egg!
6 due to popular demand

Extension activity (25 mins)

To help students develop further awareness of and confidence in paraphrasing, have them work in groups of three to write their own sentences for paraphrasing.

1. Give each group member three strips of paper. Ask each member of the group to choose and write three sentences from the Warley Woods text – each sentence on a different slip of paper.

2. The strips should be placed face down in a pile. Students take it in turns to take a strip and read out the sentence; the other group members should paraphrase the sentence.

3. Groups can then discuss which paraphrase they think is better.

Practice for the test (30 mins)

This can be done in class as pairwork or assigned for homework. Remind students to look back at the Exam tips in the unit. Point out that students can do more activities online if they want extra practice or to consolidate what they have learnt.

Answers
1 A – paragraph 6   2 A – paragraph 4   3 A – paragraph 5
4 A – paragraph 1   5 A – paragraphs 4 and 5
6 A – paragraph 5   7 C – paragraph 3   8 C – paragraph 2
9 D – paragraph 4

Listening: Living on campus

Student preparation for this class: Have students complete the Online / Workbook vocabulary preparation exercises at home before the lesson begins.

Teacher preparation: For Spot check 1, prepare three sets of cards: one set with pictures of the university services in Exercise 1 of the Workbook or Online, i.e. halls of residence, library, medical centre and sports centre; one set with the labels *halls of residence, library, medical centre, sports centre;* one set with definitions 1–4 in Exercise 2 (omit definition 5, which has no accompanying vocabulary). Prepare enough sets for students to work in groups of four. (20 mins)

Online / Workbook vocabulary preparation

▌**Focus:** The purpose of these exercises is to introduce vocabulary related to university services; provide spelling practice; practise prepositions of place.

Develop your exam skills (Student's Book p. 44)

▌**Focus:** These exercises train students to listen for detailed information about locations of facilities and to complete sentences; give short-answer questions; label plans.

Introduction

Use one of the Spot checks to clarify students' understanding of the Online / Workbook vocabulary preparation. You can use the other Spot check at an appropriate time during the lesson.

Spot check 1

To reinforce the vocabulary for university services and their definitions, use the cards you prepared before class.

1. Put students in groups of four and give each group three sets of cards: pictures, words and definitions.

2. Students shuffle the cards and place them face down.

3. Students take it in turns to choose three cards and turn them face up. They look for a match of picture, word and definition. If they get a match, they keep the set. If they do not get a match, they put all the cards back.

4. The student with the most sets wins.

Spot check 2

To reinforce students' spelling accuracy, give them a spelling quiz.

1. Put students in pairs and tell them they will be competing against other pairs.

2. Ask students to close their books. Read the following sentences from Exercise 3 of the Workbook or Online, repeating the words in italics, and ask students to spell them correctly:
   1 The lecturer told his students to read *through* the article quickly.
   2 *There* was a long queue of people waiting at the medical centre to see the doctor.
   3 The university has a number of *restaurants*.
   4 A lot of people enjoy meeting visitors from *foreign* countries.
   5 To get to the library, take the first road on the left and keep walking *until* you get to the end of the road.
   6 The tutor's office is on the *twelfth* floor.

3. Check the answers by getting students to come up and write the words on the board.

4. The pair with the most correct answers wins.

Exercise 1: Completing sentences

a) Go over the Exam information on sentence completion. Emphasize the importance of writing grammatically correct sentences when doing sentence completion, as well as correct capitalization and punctuation.

b) Point out that students should predict what they are going to hear as this will make the task easier. Tell them to cover the sentence endings in the box and complete sentences 1–6 in any way they can which is grammatically correct.

c) Put students in pairs and have them read each other's sentences to check grammatical accuracy. They can then uncover the real endings and compare answers.

Answers
1 the right   2 the corner   3 opposite   4 straight ahead of you   5 Medical Centre   6 to the lake

 ## Exercise 2: Completing sentences

a) Draw students' attention to the instruction about thinking of expressions they could expect to hear in the exercise. Remind them of the importance of predicting what they are going to listen to.

b) Elicit how many words they have to write. Then play the recording (track 31). Students complete the sentences and check in pairs.

> **Typical mistakes:** Students may write more than three words for an answer. Point out that this would lose them marks in the real exam.

Answers
1 of the wood   2 the first floor   3 round the lake
4 across the green   5 Student Union building   6 (right) next (door)

 ## Exercise 3: Short-answer questions

a) Go over the Exam information on short-answer questions. Check that students understand there is no need to change the words they hear, but highlight once again the importance of keeping to the word limit.

b) Ask students to read sentences 1–6 and then play the recording (track 32). Have them compare answers in pairs.

Answers
1 ground floor   2 meet friends   3 fourth floor   4 on campus   5 four   6 play football

 ## Exercise 4: Labelling a plan

a) Go over the Exam tip. Emphasize that the information learners hear will be in order.

b) In pairs, have students make true sentences about the facilities they can see in the picture, e.g. *The theatre is near the Students' Union*. Point out that this is preparing them for the listening exercise and they can use strategies like this in the exam.

c) Play the recording (track 33). Feed back as a class.

Answers
1 D   2 A   3 B

Extension activity (20 mins)

To provide further practice in listening for prepositions of location and labelling places, pair students up to swap plans of a university campus.

1. On the board draw a simple plan of a university campus with SHOPS (labelled) in the middle, a road and a bus stop. Ask students to copy the simple plan. Then, working individually, they should add the following campus facilities to the plan: *sports centre, lecture theatre, Business School, theatre* and *bank*.

2. Students then take it in turn to describe their plans. The student who is listening should start with a clean plan and add the facilities to it as the other student describes the campus.

3. When they have finished, they compare their plans to make sure they understood their partner correctly.

 # Practice for the test (30 mins)

This can be done in class as pairwork or assigned for homework. Remind students to look back at the Exam tips in the unit. Point out that students can do more activities online if they want extra practice or to consolidate what they have learnt.

Answers
1 A   2 B   3 E   4 C   5 online catalogue   6 a number
7 plan   8 (student) ID card   9 makes a beep / sound / (it) beeps   10 prints a ticket

UNIT 5: ARTS AND MEDIA

Writing: Films

Student preparation for this class: Have students complete the Online / Workbook language preparation exercises at home before the lesson begins.

Teacher preparation: For Spot check 1, download and copy the handout (one per student); for Spot check 2, download, copy and cut up the cards (one set of three circles per student). (20 mins)

Online / Workbook language preparation

Focus: The purpose of these exercises is to introduce common words for talking about films; introduce percentages and fractions and how to use them to describe viewing figures.

Develop your exam skills (Student's Book p. 46)

Focus: These exercises train students to read and correctly interpret pie charts: how to compare pie charts and write a summary in preparation for one of the question types in Task 1.

Introduction

1   Introduce the unit by getting students to talk about the pictures on pages 48, 52 and 53 in pairs. Ask them to talk about what they can see and how it might relate to the unit topic, *Arts & Media,* and the Speaking section, *Films.* Elicit information from students and have them guess what the other sections will be about (e.g. the photo of magazines is self-explanatory; the studio and the TV screen can relate to TV or radio or communicating information; the TV screen could be two of the previous topics).

2   Use one of the Spot checks to clarify students' understanding of the Online / Workbook language preparation. You can use the other Spot check at an appropriate time during the lesson.

Spot check 1

To reinforce understanding and recall words related to films, distribute the Spot check 1 handout and have students complete the information individually. Then put students in groups of four to discuss the films they have chosen.

Spot check 2

To provide further practice in using quantifiers, play a mingling activity.

1.   Hand out a set of three incomplete circles to each student.

2.   Ask students if they can make one complete circle from what they have. (They can't.)

3.   Tell students to ask each other for what they need, e.g. *Have you got three quarters of a circle?* If the answer is *Yes*, the other student asks for what he/she needs. If the answer is *Yes*, they exchange cards. If the answer is *No* to either question, they both find another student to ask.

Exercise 1: Understanding a pie chart

a)   Spend 2–3 minutes discussing the Exam information. Remind the students that they have already looked at pie charts in Unit 4. Ask questions, e.g.

What percentage does a complete circle represent?

What's another way of saying 'a share of the pie'? (Answer: proportion)

What does each share or proportion represent or show?

Why is it useful to see these different categories?

Are they only compared as percentages?

b)   Ask students to do the exercise following the instructions in the book and compare their answers in pairs.

c)   Follow up by asking students to identify the sentence that uses an approximate amount (sentence 4). Elicit how students can see this is less than 25% (because the angle of the share is less than 90 degrees).

Answers
2 A   3 B   4 A   5 B   6 A

Exercise 2: Giving approximations

a)   Draw attention to the Exam tip. Link this with what you discussed about item 4 in Exercise 1.

b)   Before students begin, highlight the language used to describe the categories, e.g. *13–24 years* (*between 13 and 24 years old*). Elicit how to write *55+ years* (*over 55 years old*). Highlight the example sentence.

c)   Students do the exercise individually and check their answers in pairs.

Suggested answers
Just over a third of cinema visitors are between 25 and 39. Almost 25 percent of cinema visitors are young people aged 13 to 24 years old. Just under a quarter of people who visit the cinema are between 13 and 24 years old. Nearly a third of people who visit the cinema are over 55 years old.

Exercise 3: Comparing pie charts

a)   Spend 2–3 minutes discussing the Exam information on page 47. Elicit any language the students might need, e.g. *more/less than*, *increase/decrease in/by*, *and/but*.

b)   Have them do the exercise. Draw attention in feedback to the use of *to* and *by*, an important distinction when discussing data such as that used in pie charts. Refer to the Grammar section: *Modifying adverbs used with comparisons*.

Answers

2 T 3 F 4 T 5 F 6 F 7 T 8 T 9 F 10 T

1 The pie charts show how many people watched films in different formats in 1992 and 2008.

3 Fewer people watched films on television in 2008 than in 1992. / More people watched films on television in 1992 than in 2008.

6 There was a large increase in the number of people watching films on DVD from 1992 to 2008.

9 From 1992 to 2008 the number of people watching films on television decreased by just over 50 per cent.

Exercise 4: Analysing pie charts

a) Point out that some of the gaps in Exercise 4 can have different answers. Say *a quarter* and elicit the alternative: *25%;* say *approximately* and elicit the alternative: *about*. Refer to the Grammar section: *Nouns for describing quantities in graphs and charts.*

b) Have students do the exercise in small groups and feed back as a class.

Answers

2 story **3** cost **4** a quarter / 25 per cent **5** about / approximately **6** Two thirds / 66 per cent **7** five per cent **8** proportion / number / percentage **9** approximately / about **10** per cent

Extension activity (50 mins)

Conduct a similar survey of reasons for buying films among the class and create two pie charts to serve as a writing prompt.

1. Put students in two groups, male and female, and have them conduct separate surveys into reasons for buying films. Each student in a group should give just one main reason.

2. Get each group to draw a pie chart of their findings and then discuss whether they think they are representative of a bigger sample. Have them adjust the charts to what they think is more representative.

3. Have one student from each group draw their pie charts on the board and discuss whether they are happy with the result.

4. Ask students to think about how they could use the model in Exercise 4 to write a summary. Point out that they would have to add language such as *we think/feel* at each stage of the summary.

5. Give students 20 minutes to write up their summaries following the model in Exercise 4.

Practice for the test (30 mins)

This can be done in class or assigned for homework. Suggest that students spend up to 30 minutes on the task to allow them to develop the skills they need to produce good quality work. As students become more proficient, the amount of time they spend on practice exam tasks can be gradually reduced until they can complete the work within the time allotted in the exam. Point out that students can do more activities online if they want extra practice or to consolidate what they have learnt.

Task 1

Model answer

The pie charts show the proportions of Oscar winners for seven different genres of film in 2003 and 2008. Between 2003 and 2008 the proportion of films that won Oscars changed for nearly all the genres. In particular, many more action films and science fiction films won Oscars in 2008 than in 2003. The proportion of thrillers that won Oscars went down from about half of the total in 2003 to a third in 2008. The number of horror films that won Oscars also decreased by about half from 2003 to 2008. Action, documentary and science fiction films all increased their share of Oscars between 2003 and 2008. Action films increased from about 20 per cent of the total in 2003 to almost a quarter in 2008. The proportion of Oscar winners for documentaries, romance and science fiction all increased by approximately fifty per cent between 2003 and 2008. The percentage for comedy films that won Oscars stayed the same in 2003 and 2008 at about 5 per cent.

Reading: Books

Student preparation for this class: Have students complete the Online / Workbook vocabulary preparation exercises at home before the lesson begins.

Teacher preparation: For the Extension activity, source and photocopy two texts about literature, e.g. book reviews, of an appropriate level of difficulty (200–300 words). (25 mins)

Online / Workbook vocabulary preparation

Focus: The purpose of these exercises is to introduce words for types of books and to practise deducing meanings of words by focusing on word parts, e.g. *auto-, -graphy*.

Develop your exam skills (Student's Book p. 49–51)

Focus: These exercises train students to answer exam questions that involve completing sentences with words from a passage.

Introduction

Use Spot check 1 to clarify students' understanding of the Online / Workbook vocabulary preparation. You can use Spot check 2 at an appropriate time during the lesson.

Spot check 1

To check students' understanding of vocabulary related to different genres of books.

1. Put students in two teams.

2. Write the first three or four letters of a word from Exercise 1 or 3 in the Workbook or Online on the board, e.g. *mys-*. The first team to complete the word correctly *(mystery)*, wins a point. Teams can then suggest other words that start with the same letters, e.g. *mysterious*. They get another point if they can use the words in a sentence about books or literature, e.g. *The stories in mysteries are about mysterious events.*

Spot check 2

To reinforce the vocabulary from the Workbook or Online and to extend it, do the following activity.

1. Ask the students for examples of the following:

   - nouns that relate to the Arts and that begin with *bio-* or *dia-*, or that end in *-graphy*, e.g. *biography, autobiography, dialogue, photography, bibliography*. Accept any correct answers.

   - types of books. You can help students by asking them to imagine that they are looking at their bookshelves at home or that they are in a book shop looking at the different sections, e.g. biology text books, business text books, science fiction, romance, self help guides, horror, drama, dictionaries, cook books, fantasy, biographies, children's books, books about health / architecture / photography.

2. Write 15 of the students' answers on the board. Then drill the correct pronunciation.

3. Ask students to work in pairs and write the words on the board in the correct categories. The first pair to complete the task wins.

Fiction	Non-fiction	Other
e.g. horror	e.g. books about photography	e.g. dialogue

4. Check answers as a class.

Exercises 1 and 2: Synonyms and antonyms

a) Go over the Exam information on completing sentences and draw attention to the Exam tip. Give students a few minutes to discuss whether they find synonym and antonym exercises difficult and whether they have any strategies for doing them.

b) Students do Exercises 1 and 2 individually and check their answers in pairs. Encourage them to do the

exercises without using dictionaries. As you monitor, find out and discuss any strategies students are using.

> **Typical mistakes:** Some students may be confused by words that have more than one meaning. They may also find the exercises difficult because of the number of words they do not know. Encourage them to match the more obvious pairs first, e.g. *lost* and *found*, and to guess the pairs they are uncertain about using strategies such as matching the same parts of speech.

Answers
1 d 2 a 3 f 4 g 5 c 6 b 7 e
1 d 2 a 3 e 4 c 5 f 6 b

Exercise 3: Identifying similar meaning

a) Point out that references to information in a text can use longer phrases or definitions. Explain that these are not necessarily synonyms or antonyms, but may just be different ways of referring to the same thing, as in the example. Sometimes these references explain what the more difficult words mean so they may be similar to dictionary definitions. It is important that students look for explanations in the text when they come across words or phrases they do not know.

b) Ask students to do the exercise following the instructions in the book and compare their answers in groups of three or four, checking answers in a dictionary if necessary. Monitor students while they do the task.

Answers
1 E-books, or books that are read on a digital device rather than as a print book, are growing in popularity.
2 These types of books can be read on a variety of computers or on e-readers, mobile electronic devices that are made especially for reading books.
3 E-readers are light and easy to carry, and that is just one of the advantages of these electronic devices.
4 There was a decline in sales of e-readers a few years ago, but this fall lasted only for a short while.
5 Many e-readers include software which lets readers buy and borrow e-books from libraries and shops directly; they don't have to waste time downloading them onto a computer first.

Exercise 4: Scanning for synonyms

a) Remind students of the scanning they did in Units 2 and 3 and emphasize that it is a key skill needed for the exam. Draw their attention to the Exam tip.

b) Ask students to do the exercise individually, following the instructions in the book. Give them 90 seconds to scan the text and then see how many words they managed to find. It will help if they underline each word in the text as they find it.

c) Follow up by putting students in groups and asking them to identify what helped them find the words or synonyms. Strategies may include looking for similar parts of speech, e.g. *crammed* and *full* (adjectives); similar verb forms, e.g. *stopping* and *preventing*; word parts, e.g. *re-read*; singular / plural nouns, etc. Refer to the Grammar section: *Prepositions for talking about the purpose of actions or things*.

> **Typical mistakes:** Students tend to waste time when they can't find an answer quickly. Remind them that the answers are in order and encourage them not to spend too long on words they cannot find quickly, but to come back to them after locating the rest of the words.

Answers
1 enjoy – delight in   **2** full – crammed   **3** re-read (same)
4 assemble – collect   **5** interest (same)   **6** stopping – preventing   **7** small – compact   **8** outweigh (same)
9 mobile (same)   **10** permits – allows   **11** useful – handy
12 unknown – unfamiliar   **13** worsens – declines
14 larger – bigger   **15** odd (same)

EXTENSION ACTIVITY (30 mins)
1. To provide further practice in scanning to find words in a text, ask students to select ten words from another reading text. Put students in two groups and give each group a different text that you have brought along to class.
2. Students write down the ten words they have chosen in a list to give to a student in the other group.
3. Pair up each student with someone from the other group and have them swap word lists and texts. They then work individually to try to find all the words on their partner's list in 60 seconds.
4. Have a discussion about what sort of words students selected, whether their partner found the words easy or difficult to identify in the text, and why that is. Have them think about strategies that can help to locate words, such as focusing on the first two or three letters of words as they search rather than trying to look for whole words.

Practice for the test (30 mins)

This can be done in class as pairwork or assigned for homework. Remind students to look back at the Exam tips in the unit. Point out that students can do more activities online if they want extra practice or to consolidate what they have learnt.

Answers
1 findings / scientific findings   **2** passive
3 analytical skills   **4** higher education   **5** understanding

Speaking: TV and radio programmes

> **Student preparation for this class:** Have students complete the Online / Workbook language preparation exercises at home before the lesson begins.
>
> **Teacher preparation:** None

Online / Workbook language preparation

> **Focus:** These exercises introduce language for talking about TV and radio programmes: introducing words and phrases for types of programmes; introducing words and phrases to describe programmes; focusing on adverbs of frequency; revision.

Develop your exam skills (Student's Book p. 52)

> **Focus:** These exercises focus on Part 2 of the Speaking test, where students will speak about a topic. Exercises 1–3 focus on key words and talking from notes; Exercises 4–7 focus on organizing answers and provide an opportunity for speaking practice.

Introduction
Use one of the Spot checks to clarify students' understanding of the Workbook / Online language preparation exercises. You can use the other Spot check at an appropriate time during the lesson.

Spot check 1
To check students' recall of words to describe types of programme, do the following activity.

1. Put the following table on the board:

	presenter	questions	information about things that really happen(ed)	guests	characters
game shows					
soap operas					
the news					
talk shows					
documentaries					

2. Ask students: *Which type of programme can have* (word from the top row)? Students answer with a word from the column on the left. Put a tick (✓) in the right places in the table, e.g. game shows, the news, talk shows and documentaries can have a presenter, so there should be four ticks in the *presenter* column.
3. Ask individual students questions about the words on the left, e.g. *Do you watch the news? What is your favourite soap opera?*

Spot check 2
To practise adverbs of frequency and word order, do the following activity.

1. Ask students to think about the types of television programmes they watch.
2. Show them what you want them to do by writing the following sentences on the board:

    I often watch documentaries. They are usually about animals. I sometimes watch programmes about people too. I rarely watch documentaries about places. They are always boring.

3. Ask them where the adverbs and verbs are in the sentences on the board and underline them.

4. Ask them to use the underlined adverbs of frequency to write five sentences of their own about the programmes they watch. They must make sure that all five adverbs are used.

5. Then ask students to work in pairs and to check that the sentences are correct by reading them out to each other and checking the order of the verbs and adverbs.

Exercise 1: Matching key words to model notes

a) Go over the Exam information about Part 2 of the Speaking test and then have students do the exercise individually.

b) Students discuss in pairs how the notes would help them talk without pausing as they give an organized answer. During feedback, highlight the Exam tip.

Typical mistakes: If students talk about a programme (or other topic) they like very much, they tend to get enthusiastic and pay less attention to the way they speak and to the organization of their answer. Point out that the reason for following the order on the card is to keep them focused on the task. It will also make it easier for the examiner to follow what they are saying because it is what the listener expects to hear.

Answers
type of programme: 3
favourite parts: 1
who: 5
explain what: 2
extra note: 4

Exercise 2: Assessing a Part 2 answer

a) Have students read the question in Exercise 1 again, and then discuss in groups what they think of the answer. It is important that they come to their own conclusions.

b) Elicit views and discuss as a class.

Answers
1 F – *Favourite parts* is missing.
2 F – The order in the answer is:
  • explain what you learnt: *she was from a poor family ... she had no qualifications from school ... she lived in different countries ... she now lives in her hometown and she writes there.*
  • who you watched it with: *I watched it with my classmates.*
  • type of programme: *It was a documentary and it was about a famous writer.*
3 F – The answer is out of order and incomplete.

Exercise 3: Assessing a second Part 2 answer

a) Ask a volunteer to read the example answer. Elicit a few quick opinions of what students think of the answer before doing the *True / False* tasks.

b) Have students compare their answers in pairs.

c) Discuss answers as a class. Make sure students understand what makes a good answer.

Answers
1 T 2 T 3 T

Exercise 4: Finding phrases for giving examples and organizing a text

a) Have students find the answers and then check in pairs. Refer to the Grammar section: *Using adverbs to say how often you do something.*

b) Discuss how students can incorporate this language into their own answers.

Answers
Giving examples: *A good example of this is ...; For example, ...*
Organizing your answers: *Firstly, ...; Finally, ...*

Exercise 5: Planning a Part 2 answer

a) Give students one minute to write their notes.

b) Have them discuss their notes in pairs while you go round monitoring and helping as appropriate. Point out the importance of clear, concise notes.

Typical mistakes: When making notes, students may write too much about the key words or write sentences that are too long. Giving them one minute only to plan is good practice for the exam as well as discouraging them from writing too much.

Exercise 6: Recording and assessing a Part 2 answer

a) Highlight the Exam tip. Discuss reasons why this is important.

b) If possible, have students record their answers and then listen to what they have done.

c) Give students a few minutes to identify and practise at least one way of improving their response, recording their answers if possible. Ask them to listen to their first and second attempts and note any improvements.

Extension activity (10 mins)
To provide practice in answering the Speaking test Part 3 questions.

1. Ask students to write three follow-up questions for this task card, based on what their partner said.

2. Have students ask their partners the follow-up questions and answer the questions they are asked.

Practice for the test (20–30 mins)

This can be done in class as pairwork or assigned for homework. Remind students to look back at the Exam tips in the unit. Point out that students can do more activities online if they want extra practice or to consolidate what they have learnt.

Part 1

Exercise 1
Model answers

When did you last watch television?

I watched television yesterday. I finished my homework and I watched a couple of soap operas with my friends.

What do you usually watch on television?

I usually watch reality TV shows or game shows. I sometimes watch drama series too.

What are some popular programmes in your country?

TV is very popular in my country. There are lots of channels. Soap operas are very popular. Everybody watches them.

Why do you think some TV programmes are popular?

I think soap operas are popular because we like watching characters in real life. The characters are like friends or neighbours. It's good entertainment because it's sometimes relaxing and sometimes exciting.

Listening: Communicating information

Student preparation for this class: Have students complete the Online / Workbook vocabulary preparation exercises at home before the lesson begins.

Teacher preparation: None

Online / Workbook vocabulary preparation

Focus: The purpose of these exercises is to introduce vocabulary related to crime; provide practice using collocations for crime words; provide listening practice for when words link together.

Develop your exam skills (Student's Book p. 54)

Focus: These exercises focus on thinking about question words in the Listening test and answering a range of different question types: short-answer questions, table completion and multiple choice.

Introduction
Use the Spot check to clarify students' understanding of the Online / Workbook vocabulary preparation.

Spot check
To reinforce crime words, do the following activity.

1. Ask students to draw five columns on a piece of paper with the headings *person*, *crime*, *verb*, *weapon*, *adjective*. (You will need to teach the word *weapon*.)

2. Books closed, read out the following words from the Workbook or Online: *break into, thief, shoplifter, knife, gun, gang, pickpocket, crime, burglar, dangerous, careful, steal, rob, attack, safe*

and *robber*. Ask students to write the words in the correct column. If a word does not seem to go into a column, they should write it outside the columns.

3. Put students in groups of three to compare their answers.

4. Check students' answers by asking them to come and write their answers in the correct column on the board.

5. Check the meaning of words which do not fit into the columns, e.g. *gang*.

Exercise 1: Predicting answers from key words
a) Draw students' attention to the Exam information and the Exam tip. Highlight the importance of underlining the question words and the key words in questions before they listen in the exam.

b) Ask students to underline the important words in the questions and predict the answers. Point out that you do not expect them to guess correctly, but that they should still only write a maximum of four words. Have them compare their answers in pairs.

Answers
1 <u>What</u> is the most <u>common crime</u> in the <u>UK</u>?
2 <u>What two forms of theft</u> does the policewoman mention?
3 <u>Why</u> are people in <u>more danger</u> when they are <u>abroad</u>?
4 <u>What</u> should people <u>leave</u> in the <u>hotel on holiday</u>?
5 <u>What kind</u> of <u>mobile</u> is <u>popular</u> with <u>thieves</u>?

 ### Exercise 2: Answering short-answer questions
a) Play the recording (track 37) so students can check their answers.

b) Discuss how accurate their predications were and how it helped with the listening.

> **Typical mistakes:** Students may write more than four words. Explain that they will lose marks if they do this in the exam.

Answers
1 theft   2 robbery, burglary   3 don't know country
4 passport and money   5 smartphone

 ### Exercise 3: Completing tables
a) Make sure students underline the headings and check they understand what they will write in each column (words or numbers).

b) Play the recording (track 38) and ask students to compare their answers in pairs.

Answers
USA – 911   Australia – 000   Germany – 112   India – 100

Exercise 4: Completing a table
a) Ask students to read what the security officer says and then choose the best answer, a, b or c.

b) Have them discuss their choice and the reasons for it. Don't confirm at this stage.

Typical mistakes: Students may have chosen the wrong answer because the answers are so close in meaning or wording. Point out how important it is to read very carefully and try to spot the difference between the answers.

Answer
b

Exercise 5: Understanding multiple-choice questions

a) Students read the answers and explanations. Refer to the Grammar section: *Using adverbs to say how often you do something.*

b) Have a class discussion about why students make the wrong choices in multiple-choice questions and how to avoid them.

 ### Exercise 6: Answering multiple-choice questions

a) Ask students to predict the answers before they listen and let them compare their predictions in pairs.

b) Play the recording (track 39) so that they can check their answers.

Answers
1 c   2 a   3 c   4 c

Extension activity (15 mins)
To provide further practice in listening to numbers, ask students to dictate telephone numbers to each other.

1. Have students write down five telephone numbers that they know. (They could use their mobile phones to help them if they have one.)

2. Students take it in turns to dictate their telephone numbers to their partner.

3. Make sure they check the numbers by having the second student read the number back to the first student.

 ### Practice for the test (30 mins)

This can be done in class as pairwork or assigned for homework. Remind students to look back at the Exam tips in the unit. Point out that students can do more activities online if they want extra practice or to consolidate what they have learnt.

Answers
1 India   2 handbag theft   3 Latin America   4 gun crime
5 expensive jewellery   6 lonely places   7 cash machines
8 c   9 b   10 b

UNIT 6: THE NATURAL WORLD

Speaking: The weather

Student preparation for this class: Have students complete the Online / Workbook language preparation exercises at home before the lesson begins.

Teacher preparation: Download and copy the handout for Spot check 1 (one copy for each group of three). Have enough board pens so that there is one for each group of three students. You also need something to stick paper up with. Do the same for the Spot check 2 handout (one copy for each student). (15 mins)

Online / Workbook language preparation

Focus: These exercises introduce language for talking about the weather: introducing words related to weather; introducing phrases to talk about the weather; focusing on the pronunciation of vowel sounds; focusing on the difference between *can* and *can't*; revision.

Develop your exam skills (Student's Book p. 56)

Focus: These exercises focus on Parts 1 and 2 of the Speaking test. Exercises 1–4 improve students' ability to understand general questions, to give relevant answers and to expand their answers; Exercises 5–7 focus on giving fluent and organized answers and on including extra information using relevant language.

Introduction

1   Introduce the unit by getting students to talk about the pictures on pages 58 and 60 in pairs. Ask them to try to describe the different aspects of the natural world they can see. Elicit descriptions from students as a class.

2   Use one of the Spot checks to clarify students' understanding of the Online / Workbook language preparation. You can use the other Spot check at an appropriate time during the lesson.

Spot check 1

To check students' pronunciation of words to describe weather and to help them remember the words, do the following activity.

1.   Tell students they are going to do a 'running dictation'. The first group to write all the sentences (related to the weather, months and seasons) on the board will be the winner.

2.   Put students in groups of three or four. Each group chooses a group member to write sentences on the board. The other students stand in their groups at the back of the classroom.

3.   Stick up a handout at the back of the class for each group.

4.   Ask group members to take it in turns to memorize one sentence and to go to the front of the class to tell their team member what it was. If they have forgotten something, they need to go to the back of the room again, memorize the rest and go to the front again.

5.   When the sentence is on the board, they go back to the others and touch the next person on the shoulder. This person can now start with the next sentence.

6.   Make sure you know in which order the groups finish, but end the game when all the groups are ready. You could also have students who have written the sentences on the board to read them out in turn and check for any spelling mistakes.

Spot check 2

To practise the use of *can* and *can't,* do the following activity.

1.   Give each student the handout for Spot check 2. Ask them to put the words in the right order by writing the sentences.

2.   Ask students to read their sentences out loud. Make sure that they pronounce them clearly: they need to put emphasis on the verb that follows *can* /kæn/ but when they say *can't* /kɑːnt/, the stress is on *can't* itself.

Answers

1 You can swim outside in summer.
2 In cold weather you can't go out.
3 When it's sunny, you can sit outside.
4 You can go skiing when it snows.
5 You can't play tennis outside when it is rainy.
6 The weather can change quickly in the mountains.

🎧 43 Exercise 1: Assessing Part 1 answers

a)   Go over the Exam information to remind students of Parts 1 and 2 of the Speaking test.

b)   Students do the activity before listening and checking their answers.

Answers

1 a – Answer b does not say how many seasons.
2 b – Answer a is not relevant. The question is about the season not the type of weather.
3 a – In Answer b, the speaker doesn't say how he/she feels.
4 b – In Answer a, the speaker doesn't understand the question. He/She thinks the question is *Do you like it when it's hot?*

Exercise 2: Extending Part 1 answers

a)   Draw attention to the Exam tip. Elicit a possible expansion for the first question in Exercise 1 as a class.

b) Have students follow the instructions in the book and match the expansions to the correct answers in Exercise 1.

> **Typical mistakes:** The types of questions in Exercise 1 are asked in the first part of the test and are meant to be easy. However, students are likely to be nervous at this point, which may weaken their listening skills. Tell them to try to listen to the whole question rather than just react to key words, e.g. *What do you like doing when it's hot?* is not asking how you feel about hot weather, but about what activities you like <u>doing</u>. Tell students that it is better to ask for a question to be repeated than to start talking when they only managed to hear one or two words.

Answers
1 2   2 1   3 4   4 3

Exercise 3: Answering Part 1 answers
Have students do the exercise individually and check the answers.

Exercise 4: Assessing Part 2 answers
Have students do the exercise individually and check the answers in pairs. Refer to the Grammar section: *Talking about possibility*.

Answer
2 It doesn't include extra information.

Exercise 5: Expanding Part 2 answers
a) Have students do Exercise 5 individually and then check answers in pairs.

b) During class feedback, discuss whether there could be any further expansions in the answers.

Answers
1 d   2 c   3 a   4 b

Exercise 6: Practising a Part 2 answer
a) Students work in pairs and write two more expansions.

b) Have them continue in pairs to practise giving the answer. Encourage them to read it naturally by looking at each sentence and then saying it from memory.

Possible answers
I'd like to describe my favourite type of weather. My country has three seasons and there are lots of types of weather. It's a difficult choice for me, but I think my favourite is wet weather. I prefer this to the dry weather.

Yes, wet weather is my favourite. I like going shopping when the weather is wet because the shops are all indoors. I also like cooking delicious meals for my family when there's lots of rain. My favourite meal is a traditional dish with chicken and rice.

I often experience this weather in other countries. I like travelling in Europe and I always take my umbrella with me. The wet weather lasts for a long time there. It's different from my country as the rainy season only lasts for two months. It lasts from May to June.

This weather is good for relaxing. For example, you can stay at home and just watch television. You can chat to your friends online too. I speak to my friends for two or three hours.

Exercise 7: Preparing a Part 2 answer
a) Give students time to prepare. Go round while they work, monitoring and helping as appropriate.

b) Have students work in pairs to practise answering the question.

Exercise 8: Recording and assessing a Part 2 answer
Students record their answers if possible. Then they listen to a partner's recording and discuss how they could improve it.

> **Typical mistakes:** Students' answers are often too short. This can be because of lack of vocabulary, but it can also be because they are happy that they have understood the question and want to show their understanding by giving an answer quickly. Point out that the Speaking test is not like a game show where a quick and correct answer matters. Instead, it is more like a talk show: the questions should be seen as a chance for a student to talk for a while and to show their language ability. Try practising this at the beginning of each class, e.g. when you ask students about their weekend, insist that they expand their answers. Remind them that this is a useful habit and good practice for the exam.

Extension activity (10–15 mins)
To provide further practice in answering questions about the weather, do the following activity.

1. Ask students to write down three questions they could ask each other about the weather. If they are from different countries, they could ask for descriptions of the weather and the seasons. If they are from the same country, they could focus on asking about likes and dislikes and activities.

2. Students mingle with each other and ask each other their questions. If an answer is not exactly what the they have asked for, or if they think it is too short, they should ask it again.

Practice for the test (20–30 mins)

This can be done in class as pairwork or assigned for homework. Remind students to look back at the Exam tips in the unit. Point out that students can do more activities online if they want extra practice or to consolidate what they have learnt.

Part 1

Exercise 1
Model answers
1 My country has four seasons.
2 The weather in my country is very dry. There's a rainy season in January and February.
3 I feel very sad on rainy days.
4 I like going to the beach when it's hot.

Part 2

Exercise 2

Model answer

I'd like to describe my favourite season in my country. My country has four seasons and there are lots of types of weather. I think my favourite season is spring. I prefer this to the summer. Spring lasts for about three months. It lasts from March to May. Some people think that spring is short and only lasts for about two months. Maybe this is true.

I really like the weather in spring. It's often warm but it's sometimes very hot. It's often cold too. There's lots of rain in spring. I like the different types of weather because you can't answer the question 'What's the weather like today?' We don't know! It's different from other seasons in my country because it changes quickly. On Monday it's sunny, but on Tuesday there are thunderstorms.

In summer, the weather is always hot. In autumn, the weather is usually cold and dry. In winter, it's always very cold and windy. Winter makes me feel sad.

The main reason why spring is my favourite season is because there's lots of sun and you can do sports outside or just enjoy the warm weather with friends. Spring is also the end of winter, which I don't like.

Listening: The oceans as a natural resource

Student preparation for this class: Have students complete the Online / Workbook vocabulary preparation exercises at home before the lesson begins.

Teacher preparation: Prepare definitions for the words in Exercises 1 and 2; they should be simple enough for students to understand. (20 mins)

Online / Workbook vocabulary preparation

Focus: The purpose of these exercises is to introduce language related to oceans and resources from the oceans; focus on words that sound the same but are spelt differently; focus on the language for describing trends and statistics and the adjectives, adverbs, verbs and nouns used in describing graphs.

Develop your exam skills (Student's Book p. 58)

Focus: Exercises 1 and 2 focus on how to deal with unknown words and how to guess their meaning; Exercise 3 trains students to label diagrams.

Introduction

Use the Spot check to clarify students' understanding of the Online / Workbook vocabulary preparation.

Spot check

To reinforce the vocabulary relating to ocean life and natural resources, play a class game.

1. Put all the words from Exercise 1 in the Workbook or Online on the board in random order: *natural gas, trawler, off-shore drilling, mineral resource, oil rig, net, wave power, fuel, fish farm, gas pipeline, underwater turbine.*

2. Put students in groups of three and tell them they are in a team competition.

3. Say 'number 1' and read out one of your definitions of the words without saying which word it is.

4. Students consult each other and write down the word they think is being defined. Make sure you keep a note of the number of the word you define.

5. Move on to number 2 and read the next definition. Continue until you have defined all 11 words.

6. Check the answers by asking students which word they wrote for number 1 and so on. If you have a strong class, you could ask students to try to remember the definitions you read out.

Exercise 1: Guessing the meaning of words

a) Books closed, start a class discussion about what students can do when they don't know the meaning of a word. Elicit words students don't know or are not sure of and write them on the board. Ask them how they can guess if it is a noun or an adjective, and elicit some common endings for nouns and verbs. Then ask students to open their books and read the Exam tip.

b) Have students read and discuss the example. They then read the sentences carefully and make notes on the new words in their notebooks, saying what they think the meaning is and why.

c) Have students work in groups of three to explain each word and how they guessed the meaning.

Answers
1 underwater (sub = under, marine = sea)
2 not deep (fixed rigs need to rest on the sea bed)
3 fish farming (aqua = water, culture = growing)
4 journey down (to the ocean floor), shown (has + verb), marine (= sea)

Exercise 2: Identifying parts of speech

a) Have students complete the table, putting the words in the correct column. They then discuss their answers in pairs.

b) Check students' answers in a class discussion.

Answers

Noun	Adjective	Verb
aquaculture	submarine	revealed
descent	shallow	
	marine	

Exercise 3: Labelling a diagram

a)   Vocabulary in such questions as those in Exercise 3 can be difficult, so it is important to do some preparation activities before listening. Have students work in pairs and write down as many words as they can relating to the diagram at the top of the oil rig, things they can see (e.g. *windows*, *helicopter*) or things connected with it (e.g. *ocean*, *oil worker*). Point out that they should also use words that help them describe what they see (e.g. *legs*) as such words might be used by a speaker and will help the listener label the diagram.

b)   After students have shared their words, play the recording (track 44). Give students time to think about their answers and play the recording again. Ask them to compare their answers.

Answers
1 derrick   **2** helicopter pad   **3** support tower   **4** crane

Extension activity (25 mins)

To provide further practice in guessing the meanings of words, play the definitions game.

1.   Put students in teams of four and give each team a dictionary.

2.   Students work together to choose four new words from the dictionary, ones that other students won't know, and write four definitions for each of these words; one of them should be correct and the others should be false. Monitor and help the students with their definitions.

3.   One team goes first; they write their word on the board and read their four definitions to the class, the other teams have to try and guess which definition is correct. The teams take it in turns to read their definitions.

4.   Give points to the teams who choose correctly. The winning team is the one with the most points when all the teams have given their definitions.

Practice for the test (30 mins)

This can be done in class as pairwork or assigned for homework. Remind students to look back at the Exam tips in the unit. Point out that students can do more activities online if they want extra practice or to consolidate what they have learnt.

Answers
1 1000 metres   **2** 1940s   **3** 1960   **4** 11,000 metres
5 pilot's   **6** batteries   **7** panel of lights   **8** fin   **9** surface of earth   **10** minerals for industry

Writing: Natural and unnatural processes

Student preparation for this class: Have students complete the Online / Workbook language preparation exercises at home before the lesson begins.

Teacher preparation: For Spot checks 1 and 2, download, copy and cut up resource material. For Spot check 1, prepare one set for each group of 3–4 students; for Spot check 2, prepare one set for each par of students. (15 mins)

Online / Workbook language preparation

> **Focus:** The purpose of these exercises is to introduce common words associated with the natural world; introduce the passive for describing a process.

Develop your exam skills (Student's Book p. 60)

> **Focus:** These exercises train students to describe a physical process in preparation for writing one of the question types in Task 1.

Introduction

Use one of the Spot checks to clarify students' understanding of the Online / Workbook language preparation. You can use the other Spot check at an appropriate time during the lesson.

Spot check 1
To check students' recall of words associated with the natural world, put them in small groups so they can put the images of the words in alphabetical order. To make this more interesting, you can have each group competing to finish first.

Spot check 2
To provide further practice in using the passive, have students work in pairs to complete the six sentences using the 18 phrases. Distribute a set of phrases to each pair and have them produce six passive sentences.

Exercise 1: Preparing to write about a process

a)   Spend 2–3 minutes discussing the Exam information. Ask questions, e.g.

   Why is it important in your studies that you can describe a process?

   Can you see an example diagram that illustrates a process?

   When describing a process, are all the verbs in the passive?

b)   This exercise gets students thinking logically about a process. It also provides input on how to write complete sentences in the passive from notes in preparation for Exercise 2. Have students do the exercise individually and check in pairs.

Answers
d 1   **e** 2   **b** 3   **g** 4   **f** 5   **h** 6   **a** 7   **c** 8

Exercise 2: Labelling a diagram

a)   Go through the instructions carefully. Draw attention to the two procedures for transforming the labels:

- full sentences from notes

- change from active to passive.

Point out that students should label their own diagrams in a similar way, i.e. in reduced note form with minimum use of articles and prepositions.

b) Have students complete the sentences in pairs and then check answers in small groups. When checking, they should pay particular attention to the use of articles and prepositions.

Typical mistakes: Students often use a definite article when they first mention a noun. This is a particular problem when describing a process because the items mentioned in the process might be assumed to be present, e.g. *the lava* (that we know about) *comes from a volcano*. Highlight the absence of the definite article when first mentioned in the answers to Exercise 2.

Suggested answers

2 Magma erupts from the crater at the top of the volcano.
3 The magma is changed / changes into lava.
4 An ash cloud forms above the volcano. / An ash cloud is formed above the volcano.
5 Lava flows down the side of the volcano.
6 Many trees are killed by the lava.

Exercise 3: Adding signposting language

a) Highlight the importance of the words *first*, *first of all*, etc. in sequencing a text. (Students might want to check that *firstly* can also be used.) Have students discuss the diagram in pairs and clarify anything they find unclear. Refer to the Grammar section: *Sequence adverbs*.

b) Students then work individually to complete the gapped text. Elicit answers sentence by sentence, complete with sequencing adverb.

c) Have students write more sentences to describe the process.

Answers
1 Firstly / First / First of all   2 When / After   3 then

Exercise 4
Have students complete the description individually.

Suggested answer
Rocks underneath the glacier are picked up and carried along. When the glacier reaches the bottom of the mountain, it starts to melt. The ice from the glacier turns into meltwater. Next, this meltwater becomes a river and the rocks from the glacier are deposited on the riverbed. Finally, the river flows to the sea.

Extension activity (50 mins)

Have students work in groups to produce a labelled diagram for a process of their own choice: they draw and label different parts of the process. Monitor their work, helping with any vocabulary they need. When they have completed the diagram, have them write up the process as a group. They can present their completed work to the rest of the class.

Practice for the test (25 mins)

This can be done in class or assigned for homework. Suggest that students spend up to 25 minutes on the exercise, getting closer to the time allotted in the exam. Point out that students can do more activities online if they want extra practice or to consolidate what they have learnt.

Task 1
Model answer
The diagrams show how radiation from the sun reaches the Earth and how the greenhouse effect works. The greenhouse effect happens when heat radiation from the sun is trapped inside the Earth's atmosphere.

First of all, heat radiation is produced by the sun. This radiation travels towards the Earth's atmosphere. About twenty per cent of the sun's radiation is scattered and reflected by clouds. Six per cent of the radiation is scattered by the Earth's atmosphere. Approximately twenty per cent of the radiation is absorbed by the Earth's atmosphere and by clouds. Just over half of the radiation is absorbed by the Earth. As a result, the Earth is warmed by the sun's radiation.

At night some of the Earth's heat is lost but the greenhouse gases in the atmosphere trap the heat in the atmosphere. This trapped heat makes our planet warm enough for life. However, pollution may increase the quantity of greenhouse gases in the atmosphere. More greenhouse gases trap more heat. This means the Earth becomes warmer.

Reading: Back to nature

Student preparation for this class: Have students complete the Online / Workbook vocabulary preparation exercises at home before the lesson begins. Also ask them to research the three different stages of a river on the Internet and make notes on each stage.

Teacher preparation: Photocopy the Spot check photos (one set per student). Alternatively, select four of your own pictures or electronic images of coastal landscapes. They should include the geological features covered in the lesson, e.g. the Jurassic coast in Dorset (Lyme Regis), Mediterranean cliffs and the Galapagos Islands.
(15 mins)

Online / Workbook vocabulary preparation

Focus: The purpose of these exercises is to introduce words related to the natural world; focus on linking words and practise finding the meanings of difficult or new words in texts; focus on the correct use of *in fact*.

Develop your exam skills (Student's Book p. 63–65)

Focus: These exercises train students to read a passage and then complete a diagram, flow chart or picture.

Introduction

Use the Spot check to clarify students' understanding of the Online / Workbook vocabulary preparation.

Spot check

To reinforce vocabulary related to the natural world, do the following activity.

1. Put students in groups of three.

2. Show the pictures of the coastal landscapes that you have brought in. Stick or project them onto the board and label them A, B, C and D. Alternatively, give out a photocopied handout to each student.

3. Students take it in turns to describe what they can see in one of the pictures. The other members of the group try to guess which picture they are describing.

4. Groups can then discuss which place they would like to visit.

Exercise 1: Identifying sections in a text

a) Go over the Exam information on completing diagram labels. Then have students do the exercise following the instructions in the book. Remind them to skim read the text quickly.

b) Follow up with a short discussion about what helped them find the information, e.g. topic sentences. Refer to the Grammar section: *Describing a sequence or process*.

Exercise 2: Completing a diagram

a) Draw students' attention to the Exam tip. If necessary, remind them that a flow chart is a diagram that shows a process or sequence of events using arrows to indicate the order in which things happen.

b) Ask students to do the exercise following the instructions in the book and compare their answers in pairs.

Typical mistake: Students who have difficulty with accuracy may lose marks for incorrect spelling or grammar, or may use more than the maximum number of words. Explain that it is important to read both the question and the text carefully and to make sure that the words they use are exactly the same as those in the text.

Answers

1 mud, sand or soil   **2** deeper (and deeper)   **3** rock
4 (start to) crystallize   **5** process   **6** waves, tides and currents   **7** break off

Extension activity (30 mins)

To provide further practice in completing diagrams and referring to diagrams and flow charts, have students draw and label their own flow charts or diagrams.

1. Ask students to refer to the notes they made on the different stages of rivers before the class. If you have access to the Internet, they could do additional research in the lesson.

2. Students work in pairs to draw a diagram of a river and label it with information about the different river stages.

3. Display the diagrams on the walls and have the students circulate, looking at the different diagrams.

4. Follow up with a few discussion questions:

   What makes a diagram clear and effective?

   What sort of language is used in labels and explanations?

Practice for the test (30 mins)

This can be done in class as pairwork or assigned for homework. Remind students to look back at the Exam tips in the unit. Point out that students can do more activities online if they want extra practice or to consolidate what they have learnt.

Answers

1 (green) pods   **2** drumsticks   **3** green beans
4 nutrients   **5** pickled / dried   **6** dried / pickled
7 spinach   **8** skin infections   **9** joints   **10** digestion
11 (quite) pleasant   **12** common cold   **13** delicacy

UNIT 7: EDUCATION

Writing: School, college, and university

Student preparation for this class: Have students complete the Online / Workbook language preparation exercises at home before the lesson begins.

Teacher preparation: None

Online / Workbook language preparation

Focus: The purpose of these exercises is to introduce some common words and collocations associated with education; focus on the past simple tense; practise comparative forms.

Develop your exam skills (Student's Book p. 66–68)

Focus: These exercises train students to read and write about bar charts.

Introduction

1   Introduce the unit by getting students to discuss the pictures on pages 69 and 74 in pairs. Ask them to talk about what they can see and how it relates to the unit topic: *Education*. Elicit information from students about different types of education and recycle some of the vocabulary from the Online / Workbook language preparation.

2   Use Spot check 1 to recycle education collocations and clarify students' understanding of the Online / Workbook language preparation. You can use Spot check 2 to practise comparatives at an appropriate time during the lesson.

Spot check 1

Check students' recall of verb–noun collocations related to education. Ask them to close their books. On the board write the six nouns in Exercise 2 of the Workbook or Online. Using the answer key, read out the verbs that collocate with each noun; students have to listen and guess the associated noun.

Spot check 2

To provide further practice in using comparative forms, invite students to compare males and females in the class using the forms listed in Exercise 5 of the Workbook or Online. Give an example sentence and prompts based on what you can see. For example, for the prompt *carry a rucksack*, students might *say: More females than males carry a rucksack.* Other prompts might include: *have short hair, wear glasses, use an electronic dictionary, are wearing bright colours today*.

Exercise 1: Understanding information in a bar chart

a)   Elicit what students know or remember about bar charts and line graphs. Then go over the Exam information.

b)   Have students work in pairs to complete the task and then draw their attention to the Exam tip.

c)   To consolidate students' understanding of bar charts, ask them to look at the table in Exercise 1 on page 24. Ask the following questions:

What would the left-hand vertical axis show? (Answer: number of hours)

What would the bottom or horizontal axis show? (Answer: activities)

How would the bars be shaded? (Answer: each bar would have two shades, one representing teenagers 13–15 and the other teenagers 16–18.)

Answers
1 students with pass grades   **2** subjects
3 boys and girls   **4** 2003

Exercise 2: Completing a description of a bar chart

a)   Draw attention to the Exam tip. Have students do the exercise individually and then check their answers in pairs.

b)   Explain that the language of the model answer could be used to describe other bar charts. Demonstrate by writing the first paragraph on the board and erasing the content words until only the following remains: *The bar chart shows the numbers of … in … in … . The chart groups the … according to … and divides these … into … and … . There are clear differences between the … .*

Typical mistakes: Make sure that students use the past tense. Point out that even if the information in the prompt refers to a time period in the past, Task 1 responses typically begin with the present tense. This is because the subject of each sentence is usually the figure itself (e.g. *The bar chart shows …*) or parts of it (e.g. *The horizontal axis represents …*). However, for the main body, you normally switch to the past simple tense if the information in the prompt refers to past time.

Also look out for errors with prepositions as this type of response requires a good command of a range of phrases, e.g. *number of … with …, range from … to, a difference of …, did best in …, just over/under.*

Answers
2 40 thousand   **3** 20 thousand   **4** English
5 History   **6** more   **7** Geography / Art
8 Art / Geography

Exercise 3: Describing a bar chart

a)   Erase the model you wrote on the board and focus on the first sentence of the second paragraph in Exercise 2. Elicit how you could begin a paragraph about boys. Prompt with *However* and elicit:

However, there were bigger differences in the numbers of boys achieving pass grades across the subjects.

b) Ask students to write a paragraph about boys, starting with the sentence you wrote on the board.

Model answer
However, there were bigger differences in the numbers of boys achieving pass grades across the subjects. The number of boys with pass grades ranged from the highest number of just over 70 thousand to the lowest number of just under 30 thousand, a difference of around 40 thousand. Boys did best in maths, English and science. Boys had the highest pass rate in any subject: just over 70 thousand in maths. Their lowest pass rate was in geography. Boys achieved more passes than girls in two subjects: maths and science.

Practice for the test (30 mins)

This can be done in class as pairwork or assigned for homework. Remind students to look back at the Exam tips in the unit. Point out that students can do more activities online if they want extra practice or to consolidate what they have learnt.

Task 1

Model answer
The bar chart shows the numbers (in thousands) of students who chose to study different university subjects in 2005. The numbers for each subject are divided into male and female students and show some general differences between men's and women's choice of subjects. Science and maths were the most popular choices for male students in 2005, but non-science subjects were more popular with female students. The most popular subjects for female students were subjects such as social sciences, languages, literature and humanities. Social sciences were by far the most popular subjects for women. However, very few female students chose to study mathematics and law: four and six thousand students respectively. Almost no men – only two thousand – chose to study languages and very few men chose the arts. However, just as many men as women chose to study humanities.

Speaking: University study

Student preparation for this class: Have students complete the Online / Workbook language preparation exercises at home before the lesson begins.

Teacher preparation: None

Online / Workbook language preparation

Focus: These exercises introduce language for talking about studying: introducing words associated with academic subjects; focusing on word stress; focussing on collocations; focusing on the present continuous.

Develop your exam skills (Student's Book p. 69–70)

Focus: These exercises focus on Part 2 of the Speaking test, where students speak about a topic, and Part 3, where they have a longer discussion.

Introduction
Use Spot check 1 to review the vocabulary from the Online / Workbook language preparation and focus on pronunciation. You can use Spot check 2 for additional practice of the present continuous at an appropriate time during the lesson.

Spot check 1

To check students' recall of words for academic subjects and practise their correct pronunciation, do the following activity.

1. Write the following on the board, one at a time:
   mthmtcs lw rt mdcn ngnrng chmstry hstry bsnss stds ltrtr

2. Tell students that these are words for academic subjects, but the vowels are missing. Give a point to the student who can call out the complete word first.

3. Ask students to repeat the word so everybody can hear it and give an extra point for correct pronunciation.

4. Ask more students to repeat the correct pronunciation.

Spot check 2

To practice the present continuous, do the following activity.

1. Write the following table on the board:

The present continuous			
subject		verb	rest of the sentence
1. I 2. My teacher 3. My classmates 4. My classmate and I	[not]	(think about) (live) (work) (study) (sit) (write) (do) …	… at the moment.

2. Ask students to work in pairs to write true sentences about the four subjects, using the present continuous. They can choose one of the verbs on the board or use one of their own. Give them an example sentence, e.g. *My classmate and I are doing an exercise at the moment. My teacher is not sitting down at the moment.*

3. Check the sentences, making sure that students have included the verb *to be* in its correct form.

Exercise 1: Thinking about questions at the end of Part 2

a) Go over the Exam information about the questions that complete Part 2 of the Speaking test.

b) Students read the task card and questions, and discuss in pairs whether they would find them difficult or not. Deal with any issues that arise from the discussion as a class.

c) Play the recording (track 48). Give students a few minutes to talk about which question the candidate is answering and whether the candidate gave a good answer or not.

Answer
question 2

 Exercise 2: Evaluating an answer

Give students time to read the *True / False* sentences before playing the recording again. Let them compare their answers in pairs. Refer to the Grammar section: *Adjectives*.

Answers
1 T
2 T – The answer includes friends and family and answers the question correctly.
3 T – The speaker repeats *nice* three times.

Exercise 3: Choosing adjectives

Have students work individually to do the exercise. They then compare their answers in pairs, but don't go through the answers as a class yet.

Answer
very <u>important</u> subject … it is <u>interesting</u> … get a <u>good</u> job

 Exercise 4: Using a range of adjectives

a) Play track 49 and let students check their answers.

b) Draw their attention to the Exam tip and encourage them to think of other possible adjectives that the candidate could use.

c) Elicit some ways that students can improve the range of adjectives they use in the Speaking test.

> **Typical mistakes:** Students often know that they should not repeat words but do not have the vocabulary to avoid doing this. Challenge them regularly when you hear them use words like *nice, good, OK*, etc. when they express opinions in class. Other students can help and suggest synonyms, and you could show the class how to use a thesaurus. Encourage students to write the synonyms in a vocabulary notebook.

Answers
1 T
2 T – The answer includes friends and family and answers the question correctly.
3 F – Answer 3 is different. The speaker now uses a range of vocabulary.

Exercise 5: Recording answers to questions at the end of Part 2

a) Ask students to practise answering the two questions in Exercise 1 and record their answers if possible. Refer to the Grammar section: *Verbs for talking about what is happening at the time of speaking*.

b) Have students listen to the answers they recorded and evaluate them by answering the four bulleted questions. Record their answers if possible and have them work in pairs to give each other feedback.

 Exercise 6: Listening to sample answers to Part 3 questions

a) Draw students' attention to the Exam information.

b) Ask students to do Exercise 6 individually and then check answers in pairs. You may need to play the recording twice (track 50).

c) Draw the students' attention to the Exam tip and ask for some examples of adverbs from the recording *(definitely, fortunately, unfortunately)*. Check that students are clear about the meaning of each one by asking questions, e.g.

Which one do you use to agree?

Which one shows you are happy / not happy about something?

Answers
1 c   **2** a   **3** b

Exercise 7: Recording and assessing answers to Part 3 questions

a) Have students read the assessment statements before they answer the questions. They should work in pairs and take it in turns to listen to their partner answering the questions. Ask them to record their answers if possible.

b) Encourage them to assess their own answers and then discuss their assessments with their partner to check that they agree.

> **Typical mistakes:** Students may find it difficult to give answers that are four or more sentences long. If they have problems, you can make the following suggestions.
>
> • Think about question words, especially *why*, and how they would answer them.
>
> • Include both advantages and disadvantages.
>
> • Give examples where possible.
>
> For example, the framework for question a in Exercise 6 could be:
>
> *I think it is a great idea to live with your family when you are studying.* [Why?] *Firstly, this is because they can support you.* [example] *You have someone to talk to when you are lonely or when you are having problems. Secondly, living with your family can save you time.* [example] *Someone can cook dinner for you or do your washing.* [disadvantages or exceptions] *However, sometimes living with them makes it harder*

to study [example] *especially when there are small kids in the house. Also, ...*

To provide practice in thinking about synonyms to use in Parts 2 and 3 of the Speaking test, do the following activity.

1. Put students in groups of three or four. Write the phrases in the left column of the table on the board.

2. Ask students to write as many synonyms as they can for *good* in each of the examples (some suggestions are given here on the right). The group with the highest total wins.

3. Check students' answers and discuss any differences in style and meaning.

a **good** joke	funny
a **good** story	interesting
a **good** idea	great, brilliant
a **good** answer	correct, right
a **good** day	successful, pleasant, fun
a **nice** day	pleasant, warm, fine
a **nice** hotel	welcoming, beautiful, comfortable
a **nice** t-shirt	pretty, lovely, beautiful
a **nice** boy	friendly, sweet

Practice for the test (20–30 mins)

This can be done in class as pairwork or assigned for homework. Remind students to look back at the Exam tips in the unit. Point out that students can do more activities online if they want extra practice or to consolidate what they have learnt.

Part 1

Exercise 1
Model answers
1 I'm studying literature. I'm in my second year at university now.
2 I chose literature because I love reading books and because I'd like to be a teacher.
3 Yes, the course is really interesting. I have great teachers and I like learning about new types of literature all the time.
4 That's interesting. There are lots of things I like. I think the best thing is going to lectures and learning about new topics.
5 I'm not sure. In my country, there are lots of good schools and colleges and I'd like to teach there. Or maybe I can apply for another course.

Part 2

Exercise 2
Model answer
I'm going to talk about the subject I'm studying at university. I'm studying literature. The subject is about different types of literature from different times and from different countries. For example, we learn about literature from Shakespeare's time to today's writers and modern literature. We go to the theatre to watch plays or we have seminars to talk about writers and novels. This semester we're learning about American literature, which is really interesting.

I really enjoy the subject. I love reading books and now I can read new writers and experience different literature. I enjoy giving presentations and we do this every week on my course. Then we discuss our opinions. It's good fun.

Finally, I'm interested in the subject because I like learning about different times and different places and I can learn this from literature. We can learn about the world and about people. I think language is very beautiful and I enjoy reading different styles of writing.

Exercise 3
Model answer
Yes, absolutely. I'd like to be a teacher. I'd like to work with school children and teach them about literature and about plays. I'd like a good job after my course. Or maybe I could write a book.

Part 3

Exercise 4
Model answers
1 Yes, definitely. Children love meeting people and finding about new things. Unfortunately, some schools don't have good teachers and then the children don't enjoy school. But I think they always like learning and they can learn from their family or the Internet. I enjoyed going to school when I was young.
2 Yes, absolutely. I live with my family. I enjoy living at home because I can relax and just study. For example, my parents cook meals, wash my clothes and clean my room. I can spend more time studying and I think this is good.
3 My parents went to a school in my hometown. The school is a very popular one and they enjoyed it. I went to school in another country and I didn't like living away from home. My father went to university but I don't think there were lots of universities in my country at the time. Fortunately, there are lots of universities and colleges there today. I'm visiting different universities at the moment because I'm choosing which course to study next year.
4 Yes, definitely. You can learn about a new country and meet new people and I think we learn about life. It's very exciting. It's difficult to study in another language and it's hard work. But many students have extra tuition to help them and they learn the language of the country very quickly. Then the subject is easy and life is easy. I agree there are benefits but it's hard work.

Reading: Studying abroad

Student preparation for this class: Have students complete the Online / Workbook vocabulary preparation exercises at home before the lesson begins.

Teacher preparation: For Spot check 1, prepare sets of cards with words from Exercise 4 in the Workbook or Online (one word per card). Make one set for each group of eight students. (10 mins)

Online / Workbook vocabulary preparation

Focus: The purpose of these exercises is to introduce words related to education; introduce words describing country and nationality; focus on two commonly confused words: *remember* and *remind*.

Develop your exam skills (Student's Book p. 71–73)

Focus: These exercises train students to scan for information and complete tables and flow charts.

Introduction

Use the Spot checks to reinforce understanding of the vocabulary in the Online / Workbook vocabulary preparation. They can be used to introduce the topics of levels of education and countries/nationalities at appropriate times during the lesson.

Spot check 1

To reinforce vocabulary describing level of education, do the following activity.

1. Put students in groups of eight and have them stand up. Ensure that there is sufficient space to move around the classroom.

2. Give each member of the group one of the cards with words from Exercise 4 in the Workbook or Online.

3. Each group must assemble themselves into a line from the lowest level of education (nursery school) to the highest (PhD). See which group can rank themselves in the correct order the fastest.

Spot check 2

To reinforce vocabulary for describing country, language, nationality and city, do the following activity.

Give students two minutes to revise the words in Exercise 5 in the Workbook or Online. Then ask them to close their books. Ask questions 1–5.

1. Which of the counties listed are in the Far East? (Vietnam and Japan)

2. Three of the countries all share a border. Which are they? (Germany, the Netherlands and Belgium)

3. German is spoken in Germany and in which other country? (Switzerland)

4. In which two countries is French spoken as a main language? (Belgium and Switzerland)

5. Name two university cities in Saudi Arabia. (Riyadh and Jeddah)

Exercise 1: Skim reading to identify paragraph content

a) Go over the Exam information, referring students to the flow chart on page 72 as an example. Check that students are clear about the differences between a table and a flow chart by asking questions.

b) See if students remember the difference between *skimming* and *scanning*. Direct their attention to the Exam tip.

c) Have students do the exercise following the instructions in the book. Remind them to scan the text.

Answer
Paragraph numbers: 2 and 3

Exercise 2: Scanning and completing a table

a) Have students do the exercise individually following the instructions in the book, and then compare their answers in pairs.

b) Follow up by asking students to identify what features of the text helped them to complete the exercise. Direct their attention to the second Exam tip.

Answers
Countries: Australia, the UK, the US, Germany, China, Malaysia, Japan, Russia, Nigeria, Brazil, the Netherlands, India (Note: Europe is not a country.)
People: Russel Howe, Manal
Organizations or institutions: the British Council, Stellinga International College, the faculty of Art and Design (at Stellinga)

Exercise 3: Scanning with a time limit

a) Students practise scanning for the items in the table. Remind them to allow themselves just one minute to do the task.

b) Have class feedback on whether it was easy to find all the words and whether there was anything in the text that helped them.

Answers
Numbers: *10, one, two, 5, 11th, 1*
words in italics: *needed, wanted, internationalization*
words in bold print: the title and all subheadings
abbreviations: UK, US, i.e., e.g.

Exercise 4: Scanning to focus on paragraph content

a) Students do the exercise individually. You could time them or ask the students to time themselves.

b) Have students check their answers in pairs.

Typical mistakes: Students who are reluctant to scan should be given a time limit to complete the exercise.

Answers
1 Paragraphs 2 and 3 – The quotation marks help to find this answer.
2 That it was a choice (something he <u>wanted</u> to do), and not a necessity (something he <u>needed</u> to do). The italics make it clear that he wants to emphasize this.
3 Paragraphs 1 and 4 – The first paragraph mentions *most welcoming* and talks about Germany as the country at the top of the list. In paragraph 4, the capital letter of *Germany* is easy to spot and the word *winner* appears very near.
4 Paragraph 4 – The word *internationalization* is in italics.

Exercise 5: Considering the importance of scanning in the exam
This can be done as a small group discussion. Encourage students to reflect on the importance of scanning for information in the exam so that they use the available time effectively. Refer to the Grammar section: *Present perfect.*

Extension activity (40 mins)
To help students have a better understanding of how flow charts can be used to represent processes, do the following activity.

1. Ask one half of the class to write a description of what they did to complete Spot check 1 at the beginning of the class. The other half writes a description of what they did for Exercise 6 in the Workbook or Online.
2. Pair up students from different groups and have them swap their texts.
3. Ask them to represent the information in their partner's text as a flow chart.

Practice for the test (30 mins)

This can be done in class as pairwork or assigned for homework. Remind students to look back at the Exam tips in the unit. Point out that students can do more activities online if they want extra practice or to consolidate what they have learnt.

Suggested answers
1 equivalent   **2** International Baccalaureate   **3** Personal statement   **4** 1000 words   **5** Passport   **6** Translations
7 interview   **8** on site   **9** phone   **10** successful
11 waiting list

Listening: Studying for exams

Student preparation for this class: Have students complete the Online / Workbook vocabulary exercises at home before the lesson begins.

Teacher preparation: Prepare sets of cards with adjectives from Exercises 1–3 in the Workbook or Online (one adjective on each card). Make one set for each group of three students. (15 mins)

Online / Workbook vocabulary preparation

Focus: The purpose of these exercises is to introduce vocabulary relating to studying and exams; cover adjectives and their comparative forms; contrast adjectives and adverbs.

Develop your exam skills (Student's Book p. 74–75)

Focus: These exercises focus on Section 3 of the Listening test and practise sentence completion. They train students to write grammatically correct answers and help them with the strategy of predicting before they listen.

Introduction
Use the Spot check to clarify students' understanding of the Online / Workbook vocabulary preparation.

Spot check

To reinforce making comparatives, play the following game.

1. Put students in groups of three and give each group a set of cards.
2. Ask one student in each group to shuffle the cards and lay them face down on the table.
3. Students take it in turns to turn a card face up. They must make a sentence using the adjective, e.g. *far*: *Paris is far away* … They then use the comparative form, e.g. *Paris is far away but London is further away*. If the student makes a correct sentence, they can keep the card. If they do not know the comparative form, they put the card back.
4. The student with the most cards wins.

Typical mistakes: Students may confuse adjectives and adverbs so make sure that you review these frequently in class.

Exercise 1: Matching sentence beginnings and endings
a) Draw students' attention to the Exam information and go through it.
b) Remind students about the importance of giving grammatically correct sentences.
c) Have students do Exercise 1 individually and then let them compare their answers in pairs.

Answers
1 b, d   **2** c, d   **3** a, c, d

 ### Exercise 2: Identifying different speakers
a) Draw students' attention to the Exam tip and discuss the importance of knowing who is talking. Look at the names of the speakers in Exercise 2 and ask students if they are boys' or girls' names.
b) Play the recording (track 53) and ask students to listen to check whether they got the gender correct.

c) Play the recording again for students to do the exercise. Then ask them to compare their answers in pairs.

Answers
1 B   2 D   3 A   4 C

 Exercise 3: Predicting listening content

a) Explain the importance of predicting what you will hear. Have students guess the answers before listening and let them compare their predictions.

b) Play the recording (track 54) and ask them to compare their answers.

> **Typical mistakes:** Students might write more than three words. Point out that if they do this in the test, they will lose marks.

Answers
1 revision timetable   2 in his mind
3 easier to concentrate   4 last-minute revision

 Exercise 4: Practising prediction

a) Look at the pictures in Exercise 4 and the sentences 1–4. Ask students to predict the words they will hear individually. Then ask the whole class what they think the answers will be and find out what the most popular predictions are.

b) Play the recording (track 55) and ask students to compare their answers.

Answers
1 mobile (phone) in   2 in the doors
3 to the supervisor   4 examination number

Exercise 5: Predicting the order of information

a) Books closed, introduce the topic of preparing for an exam and ask students what they do if they have an exam coming. Write sentences A–F on the board and have students read them and think about the best order.

b) Try to find the most popular first step by having students vote with a show of hands: *Who thinks A is the best thing to do first?*

c) Get students to work in pairs to see if they can agree on the order of steps together.

 Exercise 6: Completing a flow chart
Play the recording (track 56) and ask students to compare their answers.

Answers
1 F   2 E   3 A   4 C

Extension activity (20 mins)
To provide further practice in listening for information, put students in pairs. They take it in turns to listen for specific information as their partner talks about a family member.

1. Ask students to make notes in preparation for talking about a family member. Tell them they must include specific information, e.g. name, age, hair colour, hobbies.

2. Give students ten minutes to prepare for their talk. Monitor and help with language.

3. Have students take it in turns to talk whilst their partner listens for the specified information.

 Practice for the test (30 mins)

This can be done in class as pairwork or assigned for homework. Remind students to look back at the Exam tips in the unit. Point out that students can do more activities online if they want extra practice or to consolidate what they have learnt.

Answers
1 right exam paper   2 your examination number
3 the instructions   4 how long   5 several times
6 more difficult   7 know better   8 number of marks
9 (your) main ideas   10 a low mark

UNIT 8: WORK

Listening: Types of jobs

Student preparation for this class: Have students complete the Online / Workbook vocabulary preparation exercises at home before the lesson begins.

Teacher preparation: For Spot check 1, make sets of cards with words and pictures from Exercises 1 and 2 in the Workbook or Online (one item per card, 8 cards in total). Make sufficient sets for each group of three students. See Spot check 1 for more information. (15 mins)

Online / Workbook vocabulary preparation

Focus: The purpose of these exercises is to introduce vocabulary related to jobs; encourage students to think of words with similar meanings; introduce some phrasal verbs.

Develop your exam skills (Student's Book p. 76)

Focus: These exercises focus on Section 4 of the Listening test. Students have to listen to a monologue on an academic subject and to identify the topic of the talk.

Introduction

1 Introduce the unit by getting students to talk about the pictures on pages 78, 79 and 80 of the book in pairs. Ask them to say what they can see and how it relates to the unit topic, *Work,* and the Listening section, *Types of jobs*. Elicit information and recycle some of the job vocabulary from the Online / Workbook vocabulary preparation exercises.

2 Use one of the Spot checks to clarify students' understanding of the Online / Workbook vocabulary preparation. You can use the other Spot check at an appropriate time during the lesson.

Spot check 1

To reinforce job vocabulary from Exercises 1 and 2 in the Workbook or Online, do the following activity.

1. Put students in groups of three.

2. Give each group a set of the cards you have prepared and have students place them face down on the table.

3. Students take it in turn to turn two cards of their choice face up. If the cards match (e.g. the picture of the farmer with the word *farmer,* then the students should try to give a definition similar to the ones in Exercise 2: *A person who grows food is called a farmer.*

4. Students then return the cards to the table, mix them up again and continue.

5. Allow the game to continue until students are comfortably matching up pictures with jobs and producing definitions.

Spot check 2

To reinforce students' ability to recognize words with similar meanings, do the following activity.

1. Make sure that students don't look at their Workbooks. Put students in groups of three. Tell them to look at the board and work together to complete the word map you are going to draw on the board.

2. Draw the word map from Exercise 3 of the Workbook / Online on the board with the original gaps still blank. Allow students to work together to try to fill the gaps.

3. Check answers as a class and write the missing words in the gaps on the board.

Typical mistakes: Students often confuse phrasal verbs because they can be very close in meaning, e.g. *look at* and *look over*. Reassure them that phrasal verbs take time to learn and try to help them to review them regularly.

Exercise 1: Listening to introductions

a) Books closed, ask students what they know or remember about Section 4 of the Listening test. Alternatively, remind them that they will hear one person giving an academic talk. Read through the Exam tip with the students.

b) Before students listen to the recording in Exercise 2, help them to focus on phrases that introduce a topic in a talk. Introduce the phrase *Today I'm going to talk about …* and write it on the board. Ask students to work in pairs to write other phrases they know for introducing a talk. Get students to read them out to the class. Finally, get them to open their books, read the phrases in Exercise 1 and compare their phrases with the ones there.

Exercise 2: Completing notes

Play the recording (track 60) and have students do the exercise. Then do a whole class check of the answers.

Answers
1 Student societies   **2** a large corporation   **3** working outdoors   **4** institutions of further education

Exercise 3: Finding words with similar meanings

a) Highlight the useful strategy of predicting words that you might hear once you know the topic of a lecture and point out that Exercise 2 practises this strategy.

b) Ask students to do Exercise 3 individually and then check their answers in pairs.

Answers
1 clubs, associations   2 company, business   3 in the open air, outside   4 colleges, universities

 Exercise 4: Completing topic headings

a) Draw students' attention to the instructions in Exercise 4. Ask them to underline the most important word in the instructions. This is a way of getting students to focus on the fact that they should only write one word in each gap.

b) Play the recording for students to complete the sentences and then compare their answers in pairs. Do a whole class check. If necessary, play the recording again. Refer to the Grammar section: *Talking about duties and responsibilities.*

Answers
1 clubs   2 company   3 outside   4 universities

 Exercise 5: Completing notes

a) Draw students' attention to the Exam tip on page 77 and the strategy of using headings on the question sheet as a guide whilst they listen. Also emphasize what it says about the difference between fact and opinion. Ask students if they can think of any more phrases to give an opinion,
e.g. *In my opinion, I think, I believe.*

b) Get students to guess the jobs of Alice and Wei Long by looking at their pictures and the words in the exercise. If you have weaker students, you might want to give them their jobs before they listen to the recording and have them guess the missing words before they listen. Play the recording and have students check their answers in pairs.

> **Typical mistakes:** Students may write more than two words for an answer. Point out that this would lose them marks in the exam.

Answers
Alice: **1** a farm   **2** fruit   **3** chickens   **4** (the) animals
5 summer   **6** supermarkets   **7** local shops   Wei Long:
8 businessman   **9** information technology   **10** trade
11 small company   **12** computer parts
13 (a) receptionist   **14** decisions   **15** big company

Extension activity (20 mins)
To provide further practice in listening for information about people's jobs, ask students to talk about a family member or friend's job. Give them ten minutes to prepare and let them make notes and find the vocabulary they need to describe the person's work. When they are ready, put students in small groups and let them take it in turns to talk about the person and their job. The other students should listen carefully and then ask questions at the end of the talk, e.g. *Does he like his job? Where is his office?*

 Practice for the test (30 mins)

This can be done in class as pairwork or assigned for homework. Remind students to look back at the Exam tips in the unit. Point out that students can do more

activities online if they want extra practice or to consolidate what they have learnt.

Answers
1 police officer   **2** law   **3** practical   **4** training
5–7 a, c, e   **8** well-paid   **9** famous people / celebrities
10 (a) detective

Speaking: Choosing a job

> **Student preparation for this class:** Have students complete the Online / Workbook language preparation exercises at home before the lesson begins. Ask them to use a dictionary and write down definitions of words they do not know.
>
> **Teacher preparation:** None

Online / Workbook language preparation

> **Focus:** These exercises introduce language for talking about work: introducing words and phrases associated with jobs; focusing on language to describe jobs; focusing on grammar: *have to.*

Develop your exam skills (Student's Book p. 78)

> **Focus:** These exercises focus on Part 3 of the Speaking test, where students will have a longer discussion about a topic they have talked about in Part 2. Exercises 1–3 focus on answering the examiner's questions correctly; Exercises 4–10 focus on how to speak naturally, fluently and coherently

Introduction
Use Spot check 1 to review the vocabulary from the Online / Workbook language preparation for jobs and work. Use Spot check 2 for additional practice of *have to.*

> **Spot check 1**
>
> To check students' recall of language for talking about jobs and work, do the following activity.
>
> 1. Ask the class to stand up and form a circle. Get them all to clap and say *one, two, three.* After *three* (i.e. after the third clap), the first student needs to say a word or phrase related to the topic of work, e.g. *journalist, work experience.* If the student can do this, the class all clap again and after *three* the person to the left of the first student has to say a word or phrase about the topic. If a student can't think of a word, or if they repeat one that has already been said, they have to leave the circle. Play continues until only one person is left standing. That person is the winner.
>
> 2. You can ask students to look in their books afterwards to see what other words and phrases they could have included.

Spot check 2

To get students to practise *have to*, do the following activity.

Write the following on the board:

	at the age of 10		now	
	had to	not	have to	not
[teacher's name]				
-				
-				
-				

1. Complete the table with your own examples first (see the suggestion below). Explain that this is about what you have to do now and what you had to do in the past (when you were ten), and what you don't have to do now and didn't have to do then. Ask students for their own examples and write the students' names in the left column:

	at the age of 10		now	
	had to	not	have to	not
[teacher's name]	walk to school	help in the house	do the dishes	do the cooking
- Amira				
- Hang				
- Clara				
...				

2. Ask students to make sentences (verbal and/or written) with the information on the board, e.g. *When she was ten, my teacher had to walk to school but she didn't have to help in the house. Now she has to do the dishes but she doesn't have to do the cooking. When she was ten, Amira had to do lots of homework, but Hang didn't have to do homework at that age.*
   Check that students are using the correct forms of *(not) have to*.

Exercise 1: Identifying the key words in Part 3 questions

a) Go over the Exam information on page 78. Check that students have understood what *coherently* and *fluently* mean. Spend a few minutes discussing how students feel about this part of the test.

b) Have students do Exercise 1 individually and check their answers.

c) Discuss how identifying key words in questions can help them answer the Part 3 questions coherently.

Answers

1 <u>Compare</u> your <u>experience</u> of <u>finding a job</u> to your <u>parents' generation</u>.
2 Many people think that <u>work experience is the best way to learn about a job</u>. What is <u>your point of view</u>?
3 In <u>your opinion</u>, do <u>people work more now</u> than in <u>the past</u>?
4 Do <u>you</u> think companies <u>need people to travel to an office and work there</u>, or can <u>people work from home</u>?

Exercise 2: Identifying the function of Part 3 questions

Point out that not all the questions have the same function, a or b. Have students complete the exercise individually and compare their answers in pairs.

Answers

a give your opinion on an issue: 2, 4   **b** compare the past to the present: 1, 3

Exercise 3: Reading a model answer to a Part 3 question

Students do the exercise following the instructions in the book and compare their answers in pairs.

Answer

question 2

 ## Exercise 4: Useful phrases for giving thinking time

a) Draw students' attention to the Exam tip and then go through the exercise eliciting possible ways to complete the gaps, but don't confirm answers.

b) Play the recording (track 67) for students to complete the text.

c) Have students compare their answers in pairs and discuss how each phrase improves the answer.

d) Have students repeat the useful phrases and help them with their pronunciation.

> **Typical mistakes:** The useful phrases in Exercises 3 and 4 may be difficult to say correctly. Make sure students say *That's an interesting question* slowly and with the correct intonation and sentence stress, that they can pronounce the /θ/ in *think* well enough to be understood, and that they use the /əʊ/ sound in *suppose* and *pros*.

Answers

1 interesting   **2** think   **3** suppose   **b** cons
They give the speaker time to think and to relax.
They improve the answer by allowing people to speak at a natural pace and without pauses.

 ## Exercise 5: Listening to more useful phrases

a) Have students do the exercise individually and then compare answers in pairs before you check the answers as a class.

b) Have them repeat the useful phrases and help them with their pronunciation as before.

Answers

question 1
1 interesting   **2** see   **3** guess   **4** sure   **5** disadvantages

Exercise 6: Using phrases for giving thinking time

a) Give students a few minutes to prepare and rehearse their answers as a class.

b) If possible, students record their answers. Alternatively, they can work in pairs and take turns to listen to their partner's answer.

Exercise 7: Evaluating the way the phrases were used

a) Students can work in pairs, taking turns to listen to their partner's responses and to give feedback.

b) If possible, give them an opportunity to record their answers again and to listen to the second version.

Exercise 8: Listening to Part 3 questions and thinking about how to answer them

a) Highlight the Exam tip and reassure the students that it is normal to ask for questions to be repeated.

b) Students listen to the questions on the recording (track 69) and discuss their answers in pairs.

Answers

a question 1: give your opinion on an issue; question 2: compare the past to the present
b all of them

> **Typical mistakes:** Students may worry that examiners will not like it if they ask them to repeat something. Draw their attention to the Exam tip on page 79 and reassure them that in real life we often ask for information to be repeated; it is a normal part of a conversation such as the one in Part 3. Therefore, examiners will expect to be asked to repeat information when necessary. It will not go against the student; it would be much worse to give an answer that is not relevant.

Exercise 9: Giving Part 3 answers

Students listen to the recording (track 69), but encourage them to answer the questions without looking at their books or notes this time.

Exercise 10: Assessing answers

Students can work in pairs for this exercise, taking it in turn to listen to their partner's responses and to give feedback. You can ask students to give feedback to each other using questions 1–3.

Extension activity (15 mins)

To provide further practice in speaking coherently and fluently, do the following activity.

1. Write the following on the board:

Would you like to be a …	journalist?
	personal assistant?
	police officer?
	nurse?
	businessman/businesswoman?
	a teacher?
	…

I would (n't) like to be a … because … and because …

2. Tell students that in this exercise it is important that they answer the question using vocabulary to describe jobs and that they give an answer that is easy to follow and understand. They should also

speak without pauses and try not to repeat themselves. Encourage them to use the useful phrases from Exercises 3–5 to help them do this.

3. Ask a student to choose one of the questions on the board, to read it out loud and to add the name of another student at the end. That student has to give an answer to the question and then ask another student a new question.

4. Give feedback on the fluency and coherence of students' answers.

Practice for the test (20–30 mins)

This can be done in class as pairwork or assigned for homework. Refer to the Grammar section: *Talking about duties and responsibilities*. Point out that students can do more activities online if they want extra practice or to consolidate what they have learnt.

Part 1

Exercise 1
Model answers
1 I'm a nurse. I work in a hospital near my home.
2 Yes, I enjoy my work. My job is great because I help people every day.
3 No, I don't think so. Maybe I can train as a chef because I like cooking.
4 I work for a private hospital. It's very well known in my country and it's a friendly place to work. We get lots of training and we can work flexible hours. It's a good company.
5 Well, I work different shifts so I start work at different times. I get to the hospital and I talk to the other nurses about what we have to do that day. Then we visit all the patients and help them. I prepare food and medicine for the doctors.

Part 2

Exercise 2
Model answer
I'd like to talk about a job I had in the past. When I was at college, I worked in an office as a receptionist.

I got the job because I applied for it. I saw an advert on a college notice board for a temporary receptionist. It was well paid and the office was near the college. I emailed my CV and then I visited the office for an interview.

The job involved computer work and talking to people on the telephone. I liked using my languages and I enjoyed working with different people. I had to organize meetings and prepare reports. I sometimes visited another office and worked there.

I wanted the job because it was well paid and I could save for a holiday. I also got work experience in a busy and exciting company and I think that's important. I learnt a lot.

Finally, I did the job well. They gave me a good report for my college and they also bought me some flowers and a card to say thank you. I'd like to work there again.

Exercise 3

Model answer
My colleagues were really nice. They were very friendly and helpful. My boss was friendly too.

Part 3

Exercise 4

Model answers
1 That's an interesting question. In my opinion, I don't think it's a good idea for families to work together. For example, I have to work very hard in my job and I often feel sad or angry. But then I go home to my family and it's OK. It would be difficult if I had an argument with my family at work and then the argument continued at home.

2 Maybe. I think that work experience is very useful and you can learn a lot about the job. For example, maybe you don't like the job and want to look for a different career. I think it's also important to get a qualification and to go to college, and then you can learn about the background of the job.

3 Yes, definitely. We have computers and mobile phones and lots of people work from home today. It's normal. In the past, I think people travelled to a company and worked there, and then went home. All the work was done in the company. Today the world is very busy and people work more in their free time because they need money.

4 I'm not sure. I think it's a relaxing way to do a job because there aren't any noisy colleagues there. You can work flexible hours too, which is good. But you need a big house and a desk and equipment, so it's difficult and expensive. Maybe it's a good idea to work at home for a day or two days but not every day.

Reading: Communication at work

Student preparation for this class: Have students complete the Online / Workbook language preparation exercises at home before the lesson begins.

Teacher preparation: For Spot check 2, collect five or six interesting or well-known English advertising slogans (or use the ones given in the Spot check). Choose slogans that include the definite, indefinite or zero article. For the Extension activity, select two short news items from the Internet or local newspaper (approximately 200 words) and label them A and B. Download and copy enough for each student to have a copy of either A or B. (30 mins)

Online / Workbook language preparation

Focus: The purpose of these exercises is to introduce words and collocations relating to communication

and advertising; focus on correct use of the definite and indefinite articles *(the, a/an)*.

Develop your exam skills (Student's Book p. 80)

Focus: These exercises train students to answer exam questions that involve completing a summary of or notes about a text.

Introduction
Use the Spot checks to review the Online / Workbook language preparation exercises.

Spot check 1
To reinforce vocabulary related to advertising, do the following activity.

1. Ask students to think of an interesting slogan, logo or advertisement they have seen recently.

2. Put students in groups of three or four. They take it in turns to draw the logo, say the slogan or describe the advert for the other students in the group to guess.

3. When they have finished, have them discuss where they see advertisements and what types they think are most effective.

Spot check 2

1. Dictate the advertising slogans that you collected before the lesson, or use the following:

A diamond is forever. (De Beers diamonds)
It's the real thing. (Coca-Cola)
The best to you each morning. (Kellogg's Corn Flakes)
We keep your promises. (DHL (couriers))
Use natural speech, including contractions and weak forms.

2. Students underline all the articles in the sentences. They work in pairs to check they have written the slogans correctly and think about why there are definite, indefinite or no articles in each one.

Exercise 1: Identifying parts of speech
a) Go over the Exam information on completing notes and summaries and draw attention to the Exam tip.

b) Students complete the table individually and compare their answers in pairs.

c) Give feedback to the class and tell them that identifying the correct part of speech will help them complete the exercises in the rest of the unit.

Answers
adjectives: mobile, fast, free, speedy, handy, commercial
nouns*: satellite, mobile, newspaper, transfer, broadband, consumer, access, keyboard, signal, commercial
verbs: transfer, access, free, signal
adverbs: fast

*Note: These nouns can also be used in front of other nouns e.g. *newspaper ad*.

Exercise 2: Using clues in gapped texts to predict answers

a) Ask students to do the exercise following the instructions in the book and compare their answers in pairs.

b) Highlight and explain any language patterns that students are uncertain about. Point out that Exercise 2 encourages them to use grammatical clues to predict the missing word and is useful preparation for Exercise 3.

Answers
2 verb e.g. *return*
3 verb ending in *-ing,* e.g. *communicating;* past participle, e.g. *communicated*
4 adjective (in comparative form), e.g. *better – clear* would not be possible as the comparative form for one-syllable adjectives ends in *-er*: *clearer,* not *more clear*
5 verb, e.g. *store;* adjective, e.g. *accurate*
6 preposition: *into*

Exercise 3: Completing notes

Students complete the notes individually and then check answers in pairs. Encourage them to skim the text before they choose the missing words. Emphasize that the missing words are all in the text.

Answers
1 spoken **2** written **3** non-verbal

Exercise 4: Completing a summary

a) Have students read the instructions for this exercise carefully. They should complete the exercise individually and compare answers in pairs or groups.

b) Have a class discussion about what helped them choose the correct answers.

> **Typical mistakes:** Students may find it hard to find the correct word to complete a gap in the summary, particularly if the information comes in a different order to the text. This is why it is important to skim the text first. Also, the words surrounding the missing word may be different, e.g. *the business world* is used in the text but the summary refers to *a business environment*. Remind students that although the missing words should be from the text, the summary may contain synonyms for some of the key terms in the text.

Answers
1 business **2** layout **3** informal **4** financial **5** reports
6 standard

Extension activity (30 mins)

1. To provide further practice in predicting missing words in a gapped sentence or paragraph, have students test each other in groups of three. One student should choose a short text to read aloud, but should pause half-way through some of the

sentences for the other group members to guess the next word.

2. To encourage better understanding of gapped texts, put students in two groups, A and B, and give each group copies of the news items that you prepared before the class. Have students read the news item and blank out five words to create their own gapped texts. As and Bs should then swap texts and try to guess the blanked-out words in the text they have been given.

Practice for the test (30 mins)

This can be done in class as pairwork or assigned for homework. Remind students to look back at the Exam tips in the unit. Point out that students can do more activities online if they want extra practice or to consolidate what they have learnt.

Answers

Exercise 1
1 relatively few speak a second language fluently
2 communication problems
3 effective writing and reading skills
4 customers, suppliers, trade union officials, government officials, the local community

Exercise 2
Summary A: **1** participants **2** plan **3** time **4** achieve
5 future
Summary B: **6** necessary **7** effective **8** employees
9 preventing

Writing: Technology at work

> **Student preparation for this class:** Have students complete the Online / Workbook language preparation exercises at home before the lesson begins.
>
> **Teacher preparation:** For Spot check 1, download and copy one handout for each student. (10 mins)

Online / Workbook language preparation

> **Focus:** The purpose of these exercises is to introduce common words used in IT; introduce how to connect ideas that agree or contrast.

Develop your exam skills (Student's Book p. 83)

> **Focus:** These exercises train students to write paragraphs that evaluate questions or arguments by focusing on advantages and disadvantages in preparation for writing a Task 2 essay.

Introduction
Use Spot check 1 to review linking words and recycle vocabulary from the Online / Workbook language preparation exercises.

Spot check

To provide further practice in using common IT vocabulary and to remind students how to add ideas that agree or contrast, distribute the Spot check 1 handout. Students work individually and match the descriptions with the computer and mobile technology described. Then put students in groups of four and have them discuss whether they agree with the points made in the handout. (Answers: 1 f, 2 e, 3 c, 4 b, 5 d and 6 a)

Exercise 1: Stating advantages and disadvantages

a) Go over the Exam information. Ask questions, e.g.

   Should you focus on one side of the argument?

   What does it show if you consider both sides of the argument?

   What should you do if you believe strongly in one side of the argument? (put yourself in someone else's shoes)

b) Ask students to do the exercise following the instructions in the book and compare their answers in pairs.

c) Follow up by asking students to identify which opinions they agree with. Then have them think of a possible counter-argument so they can experience giving views that they do not share.

> **Typical mistakes:** Students often feel they should only say what they think or believe. However, it is not only appropriate but also helpful to provide different points of view. In this way they will find they have more to talk about.

Answers
1 A **2** D **3** D **4** D **5** A **6** D **7** A **8** A

Exercise 2: Matching main ideas with supporting information

a) Explain that part of having balanced opinions is being able to justify or support them. Remind students that they did work on this in Unit 1 when they looked at main ideas and supporting ideas.

b) Have students do the exercise individually. Encourage them to think about whether they agree with the supporting arguments as they do the activity. Give them time to discuss their views in pairs.

Answer
1 e **2** a **3** d / f **4** b **5** d / b **6** c

Exercise 3: Ordering ideas in a paragraph

a) Go through the six headings on the left. Explain that the main idea is always first but the others will depend on the writer. For example, you might follow a main idea with a supporting idea or an example.

b) Have students work in groups of three or four to match the headings. Then have them work together to put the headings in the best order to form a paragraph.

Answers
2 c **3** f **4** a **5** b **6** d
Best sentence order: e, a, b, c, d, f

> **Typical mistakes:** Students often feel they don't have enough to write about. By focusing on the structure of an essay, you can demonstrate how it is possible to write a lot by developing one simple idea using paragraph functions. They can vary slightly in order but always begin with the main idea, e.g. main idea, example, supporting idea, expansion, reason, etc.

Exercise 4: Organizing advantages and disadvantages

a) Draw attention to the Exam tip. Point out that this is a clear and simple way of structuring an essay.

b) Have students complete the exercise and explain that this is good preparation for Exercise 5.

Answers
Advantages: 2, 3, 5, 7
Disadvantages: 1, 4, 6, 8

Exercise 5: Writing about advantages and disadvantages

Have students write the two paragraphs and compare their writing in pairs. During feedback, briefly discuss whether they agree that these are balanced opinions.

Model answer
There are many advantages of social networking. Firstly, social networking means that people can keep in touch with their friends and family easily. For example, if a person has relatives in another country, they can keep in contact using Facebook. In addition, social networking helps people pass on news. Often when a news story breaks, social websites help us hear the experiences and opinions of the people where the news is happening.

However, social networking also has some disadvantages. Social networking can be addictive, especially in young people. They may spend too much time social networking compared to other activities. Furthermore, nobody knows the true identity of some of the people using social networking websites. People may think they are talking online to someone friendly, but it might be a dangerous stranger.

Exercise 6: Thinking of advantages and disadvantages

a) Draw attention to the Exam tip to remind students that their ideas need to be connected when they write full paragraphs.

b) Go over the three essay questions and highlight that each one is evaluative and will involve putting the advantages and disadvantages of the three issues. Go over the first one on the board to give a model of how to make notes and help students start thinking about the task. For example, elicit the following ideas, and then write them in note form (shown in brackets):

   They can make presentations more interesting. (presentations more interesting)
   You can work with computer programs as a large group. (computer programmes / large groups)

They can be connected to the Internet for many different purposes. (connect to Internet / many purposes)

c) Point out that essays 2 and 3 ask for agreement or disagreement; students highlight advantages and disadvantages to back up their argument. Tell them to work in pairs and complete notes for the other two essay titles.

> **Typical mistakes:** Most students, whether native or non-native speakers of English, have problems making notes. As it is a very useful writing skill, it is useful to give them practice each time they are asked to make notes. Highlight the fact that once they have written the content (in note form) they can concentrate on how it is written, i.e. accuracy.

Suggested answers

1 Advantages: presentations more interesting; computer programmes / large groups; connect to Internet / many purposes; flexible
Disadvantages: too much information; can waste time; staff need training; possible breakdown
2 Agree: saves time; better for communication; exciting; information easier to obtain
Disagree: takes up time; addictive; high cost; technological problems
3 Agree: learn to use more quickly; more need to learn; flexible entertainment / busy lives; some old people unwilling to learn; old people have need to get out and meet others
Disagree: have less time to waste; some websites unsuitable for very young; encourages lazy habits; young and old need information and relaxation; old people need new skills; old people / more need to communicate with others

Exercise 7: Adding a paragraph to an opinion essay

a) Draw attention to the Exam tip on page 86. Then have students read the introduction and conclusion to the essay. Elicit the opinion of the writer on using social networking sites at work. Establish that paragraph 2 presents the disadvantages and paragraph 3 will present the advantages.

b) Have students work in pairs to make notes and then write paragraph 3 individually.

Model answer

On the other hand, these sites can also have positive aspects in the workplace. Social networking isn't limited to sites like Facebook or BeBo. There are also work-based social networking sites that can be beneficial to companies. For example, LinkedIn lets professional people link up with other business people and develop their work contacts. This may bring benefits to a business. In addition, social networking can make people happier at work. Without access to things like Facebook, experienced staff might become unhappy in their jobs and decide to leave.

Practice for the test (45 mins)

This can be done in class as pairwork or assigned for homework. Remind students to look back at the Exam tips in the unit. Point out that students can do more activities online if they want extra practice or to consolidate what they have learnt.

Task 2
Model answer
Since its development in the 1970s, the Internet has become a key tool for obtaining information and for communication all over the world. The Internet has both advantages and disadvantages but overall, I believe the advantages are greater than the disadvantages.

Firstly, the Internet has made work and social life much easier. Email and using video conferencing in the workplace have made business quicker and more efficient. For example, in the past, people often had to travel long distances for meetings, but now they can video call instead. Also, the Internet makes it easier to keep in contact with family and friends through email and social networking websites. People can give friends and relatives their news quickly and easily. In addition, meetings, parties and social events for large groups of people are easier to organize in this way. Finally, finding out information online is much quicker than visiting libraries or making expensive phone calls.

On the other hand, people claim the Internet has disadvantages. Some people say that the Internet has made people lazy. For example, people now do lots of things online, like shopping and socializing, when it might be better for them to do these things in the 'real' world. Furthermore, the Internet contains a lot of information that is not correct. This is because anyone can put anything they want on the Internet and it is not always checked for accuracy or truth. Users need to be sure that the websites they look at are reliable sources of information.

In conclusion, although it has advantages and disadvantages, the Internet has made life so much easier in so many ways that as long as people know how to use it effectively, it can be an excellent tool.

UNIT 9: HOLIDAYS AND TRAVEL

Speaking: Types of holidays

Student preparation for this class: Have students complete the Online / Workbook language preparation exercises at home before the lesson begins.

Teacher preparation: Download and copy the handout for Spot check 1. Cut it up so that there is one set of words for each team. (10 mins)

Online / Workbook language preparation

Focus: These exercises introduce language for talking about holidays and travel: introducing words and phrases associated with holidays; focusing on language to describe holidays and travel; focusing on grammar: *be going to*; practising pronunciation: unstressed syllables and sentence stress.

Develop your exam skills (Student's Book p. 86)

Focus: These exercises focus on Parts 1, 2 and 3 of the Speaking test. Exercises 1–8 focus on using a range of vocabulary; Exercises 9 focuses on useful phrases.

Introduction

1   Introduce the unit by getting students to talk about the pictures on pages 87 and 89 in pairs. Ask them to say what they can see and how they think each picture relates to the unit. Ask them which are connected to the Speaking topic, *Types of holidays*. Encourage students to speculate about the landscape photo and decide where they think it could be.

2   Use Spot check 1 to review the holiday vocabulary from the Online / Workbook language preparation. You can follow this up with Spot check 2, which focuses on grammar and Spot check 3, which helps with pronunciation.

Spot check 1

To check students' recall of vocabulary associated with holidays, do the following activity.

1.   Put students in two teams and ask them to sit with their team members with books closed.

2.   Tell them they will play a game in which they have to guess types of holidays.

3.   Show a team member from the first team a word from the handout and ask them to draw a picture on the board to describe it. They cannot write any words, say anything or use gestures.

4.   Their team has one minute to guess what they have drawn. If their team can't guess the correct word, the other team can try. Give one point per correct guess.

5.   Teams take it in turns to send a member to the board. The winning team is the one with most points.

Spot check 2

At the end of the game (Spot check 1), practise the pronunciation of the types of holidays with the whole class.

Check students' ability to use *be going to* and *I'd like to*.

1.   Ask students to talk about their holiday plans in pairs, using *going to*. They can use the table in Exercise 6 that they have filled in, and add other examples, e.g. *I'm going to visit local festivals. I'm going to sit on the beach*.

2.   Ask some students to repeat their holiday plans for the whole group. Write some of their sentences with *I'm going to* on the board.

3.   Ask if they have holiday plans for next year (or the year after) yet; most students probably won't have clear plans. Ask students who say they have no plans for next year what they would like to do. Check that they are using *I'd like to* and not *I'm going to* for hopes. Write some of their sentences with *I'd like to* on the board.

Exercise 1: Matching topics to key words

a)   Go over the Exam information on page 86. Ask students to suggest some topics that might be covered in the IELTS exam, e.g. family, free time, special occasions. Have students read the list of topics and key words in Exercise 1 and establish that these words are relevant vocabulary.

b)   Have students do Exercise 1 individually and compare answers in pairs. Check the pronunciation of the answers.

c)   Put three of the words on the board, e.g. *accommodation, colleague, parade*, and ask students to write one sentence for each word. The sentences have to show understanding of the word. Ask students to read out one of their sentences.

Answers
1 g   **2** e   **3** f   **4** b   **5** a   **6** h   **7** d   **8** c

Exercise 2: Using vocabulary from Exercise 1

a)   Draw students' attention to the Exam tip. Elicit any techniques that students use to help remember and recycle vocabulary.

b)   Have students do Exercise 2 in pairs without writing any sentences. If possible, have them record themselves.

Typical mistakes: Students sometimes don't have a strategy for learning vocabulary. This is a good time to help them with this. If students had difficulty using the words in a sentence in Exercise 1, tell them that it is important that they write new words in a notebook, with an example sentence in English. Ask them how they make notes of new vocabulary and study it and how often they study. Give them advice about organized note-making and about studying little and often.

Extension activity (20 mins)

To raise awareness of the importance of vocabulary learning and revise some topic vocabulary, do the following activity.

1. Ask students to revise vocabulary from Units 1–9 for homework and to be ready for a test. You could ask them to use the Glossary at the back of the book. Tell them they will need to be able to use the words in a sentence of their own.

2. In the next lesson, you could give students a written test by dictating ten of the words and asking them to use each word in a sentence. Alternatively, you could check the meaning of the words verbally. Write words on the board and ask individual students to choose one, pronounce it and use it in a sentence.

Exercise 3: Using a wider range of vocabulary

a) Encourage students to assess their recorded answers and then discuss their assessments with their partner to check that they agree.

b) Have them repeat the activity and re-record themselves if possible.

Exercise 4: Planning a Part 2 answer using a range of vocabulary

Draw the students' attention to the Exam tip before they plan their answers. Have them work individually. Refer to the Grammar section: *Sequence adverbs.*

Exercise 5: Recording and evaluating a Part 2 answer

Ask students to do Exercise 5 in pairs, listening to each other and recording their answers if possible. Help them with vocabulary and pronunciation.

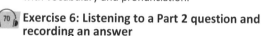 ### Exercise 6: Listening to a Part 2 question and recording an answer

Students do the exercise following the instructions in the book. If possible, record their answers and/or have them compare their answers in pairs.

Exercise 7: Identifying the function of Part 3 questions

Students do Exercise 7 individually following the instructions in the book. Refer to the Grammar section: *Talking about past situations and habits.*

Answers
1 C   2 O   3 O   4 C

Exercise 8: Reviewing useful phrases

Remind students that these useful phrases can be used to allow thinking time. Help with pronunciation if necessary and see if students can suggest some more phrases.

 ### Exercise 9: Recording answers to Part 3 questions

Ask students to do Exercise 9 in pairs, helping each other and recording their answers if possible. Help them with vocabulary and pronunciation.

> **Typical mistakes:** Questions 1 and 4 ask students to compare the present and the past. This requires them to use a mixture of present and past tenses. Remind them of this beforehand and check that they use the correct tenses. As students often use the present tense where they should use the past, listen out for this. You could tell them you will pull your right hand toward your right shoulder, to indicate the past – this way you don't need to stop them talking and they can correct themselves.

Extension activity (30 mins)

To provide further speaking opportunities and to practise using a wide range of vocabulary about a topic, do the following activity.

1. Put students in two groups: Group 1 and Group 2. Tell them that they are going to have a five-minute group discussion. Group 1 will have to talk about Question 2 from Track 73 and Group 2 about Question 3.

2. Write these questions on the board:

    Group 1: Many people think it is a good idea to go on holiday in your own country. Do you agree?

    Group 2: In your opinion, is it important to speak the language of the country you are visiting?

3. Give the groups five minutes to prepare. They need to use the time to come up with some ideas and with relevant words and phrases before they start. They also need to decide what role they will take: about half of the group need to agree with the question and the other half need to disagree (they may have to 'act' this). This will make for a more lively discussion.

4. Ask each group to debate while the other group listens. Ask each group to give feedback to the other one about vocabulary and phrases used.

 ## Practice for the test (20–30 mins)

This can be done in class as pairwork or assigned for homework. Remind students to look back at the Exam tips in the unit. Point out that students can do more activities online if they want extra practice or to consolidate what they have learnt.

Part 1

Exercise 1

Model answers

1 My last holiday was last winter. I went on a family holiday to Australia.
2 Yes, I like travelling. I like visiting new countries or new places in my country, but I don't enjoy flying.

3 I like visiting friendly cities. I enjoy meeting new people and making new friends. I like old cities with traditional restaurants.
4 That's an interesting question. Yes, I'd like to visit Canada. I'd like to go skiing there.
5 No, I don't think so. Sadly, it's very expensive and the weather is bad. There are lots of tourist attractions and historical sites but the weather is always bad.

Part 2

Exercise 2
Model answers
I'd like to talk about a special holiday I went on about two years ago. It was a learning holiday with my school.

Ten people from my class went to London in England and we went to take an English course at a university. It was about two years ago and it was in the summer. The course lasted for three weeks. We stayed in university halls and the beds were very uncomfortable.

We did lots of things. First of all, we studied very hard but we made lots of new friends. At the weekends, we went sightseeing and we visited tourist attractions. There are lots of beautiful places in London. I really enjoyed visiting the historical sites and going to the art galleries. We learnt new sports in the evenings. For example, we played cricket and rugby. Another thing we did was go on a day trip to Stratford to see a play by Shakespeare. It was a beautiful city but I didn't understand the play. We had an exam on the last day and thankfully I passed.

Finally, it's a special holiday because it was the first time I went on holiday without my family. It was also the first time I visited England and practised my English. It was very exciting.

Exercise 3
Model answer
Yes, I'm going to do a language programme next year. I'm going to America and I'm going to work in a school for work experience.

Part 3

Exercise 4
Model answers
1 I think travelling is very easy for my generation. It's cheap and quick to buy tickets on the Internet and lots of people travel every day for work or for holidays. But for my parents' generation, I think tickets were expensive and travelling wasn't very common. I don't think people went on long holidays to different countries, I think they probably stayed in their own country.
2 Yes, absolutely. My country is beautiful and the people are very friendly. Tourists come to my country every day so I think it's a good idea for us to visit the different areas of the country too. You can learn more about your country and its history and you can try local food or visit ancient ruins. I think it's a good idea.

3 That's interesting. I'm not sure. Most hotels or businesses speak lots of different languages so it's not important. Tourist attractions have guides that translate too. But it's polite to speak the language and to understand the people. I think it makes the visit more interesting.
4 Yes, absolutely. My favourite holidays or day trips are with my friends. Fortunately, we all have the same interests and like doing the same things, so we can have a great time. I think it's nice to share experiences and take photos. It makes the trip special.

Writing: Where people go on holiday

> **Student preparation for this class:** Have students complete the Online / Workbook language preparation exercises at home before the lesson begins.
>
> **Teacher preparation:** Download and copy the Spot check 1 cards. Prepare one set of cards for each group of 3–4 students. (15 mins)

Online / Workbook language preparation

> **Focus:** The purpose of the exercises is to introduce verbs (infinitive and past form) and their noun equivalent to describe changes in graphs; introduce adjectives and adverbs to describe different degrees of changes or trends; introduce ways of describing time periods used on graphs.

Develop your exam skills (Student's Book p. 88)

> **Focus:** These exercises train students to read and interpret line graphs and summarize the information. Exercise 3 shows how to write a summary based on a graph in preparation for one of the question types in Task 1.

Introduction
Use Spot check 1 to practise collocations connected to line graphs and reinforce the Online / Workbook language preparation. Use Spot check 2 to focus on time phrases at an appropriate point in the lesson.

> **Spot check 1**
>
> To reinforce use of 'adjective + noun' and 'verb + adverb' combinations, play pelmanism in groups of 3–4. Distribute the Spot check word cards to each group and do the following activity.
>
> 1. On the board, write *Tourism increased* and *There was an increase in tourism*. Highlight the use of the verb *increased* and the noun *an increase*. Then demonstrate pelmanism on the board using four large cards with the words *to drop*, *a rise*, *sharply* and *sharp* attached face down on the board. Turn over *to drop* and *sharp*. Indicate that the verb and the adjective cannot be used together. Turn the card face down again and turn over *to rise* and *sharply*. Say: *Tourism rose*

sharply. Then take the two cards off the board and put them on the table. Turn over the remaining two cards, *a rise* and *sharp,* elicit that they go together and write the sentence: *There was a sharp rise in tourism.* The student who will say a correct sentence keeps the pair of cards.

2. Students now play in groups of 3–4, collecting matching cards. To win a pair, students must:

    - pick up a matching pair.
    - make a sentence similar to the one on the board.

    If a student picks up a matching pair and fails to make a correct sentence, the cards are replaced face down.

Spot check 2

To provide practice in distinguishing between points of time and periods of time using time phrases, do the following activity.

1. Tell students to listen and watch. Say a period of time, e.g. *for ten years,* and indicate that it is a period by placing your hands apart. Say a point in time, e.g. *twenty years ago,* and indicate that it is a point by raising your index finger on one hand.

2. Say different time phrases and get students to respond with the appropriate gesture.

3. Tell students to refer to the time phrases in Exercise 5 in the Workbook / Online and elicit different times, e.g. *between 1985 and 2003* (or write them on the board to check pronunciation). Make sure they are able to say dates accurately. Have students work in pairs, taking turns to say dates while their partner responds with an appropriate gesture.

Exercise 1: Interpreting a line graph

a) Spend 2–3 minutes discussing the Exam information on page 88. Ask questions, e.g.

    Which axis of the graph shows quantities?

    Give an example of a quantity.

    What does the horizontal axis show?

    Give examples of units of time that can be shown.

    As well as an increase, what trends can a line on a graph show?

b) Ask students to do the exercise following the instructions in the book and compare their answers in pairs.

c) Follow up by eliciting true answers for 3 and 6. If the students are interested, have them briefly discuss what they think of these trends and why they are happening.

d) Draw attention to the Exam tip. If students are uncertain about how the tenses are used, draw their attention to the examples of different tenses in Exercise 1 and ask questions, e.g. *Which sentence uses the present perfect?* (item 5) Point out that students should make use of these ready-made expressions in their writing.

Answers
1 T   2 T   3 F   4 F   5 T   6 F

Exercise 2: Completing sentences that describe a line graph

Students do the exercise individually and check their answers in pairs.

> **Typical mistakes:** Students often confuse talking about the graph with what it shows. When talking about the graph, we use the present simple; when talking about what it shows, we use a tense that relates to the time on the horizontal axis: past, present or future.

Answers
1 shows   2 dropped   3 went down   4 will stay

Exercise 3: Completing a description of a line graph

a) Have students do the exercise in small groups. Encourage them to discuss each of their answers and the reasons for their choice.

b) Have whole class feedback and discuss the structure of the text:

    - what the graph shows
    - a general comment about Singapore
    - specific numbers for Singapore
    - a general comment for Japan and Thailand (because the graphs are similar)
    - specific numbers for Japan and Thailand
    - a comment on the similarity of the figures
    - a commentary on the direction of the graph

    Point out that there is a clear structure.

> **Typical mistakes:** Students don't always understand the importance of variety in their writing. For example, they will overuse *rise* rather than including *go up* and *increase.* Similarly, they often fail to make use of adjectives and adverbs to signal different degrees of change in a graph.

Answers
1 shows   2 visited   3 went   4 between   5 fluctuated
6 travelled   7 dropped   8 rose   9 in   10 see   11 was
12 remained   13 increased

Extension activity (50 mins)

Conduct a survey of tourism in different countries around the world. Agree a time period, e.g. 2009–2013 and have different students choose a country and draw a graph about a particular topic. (See, for example, http://data.worldbank.org/indicator/ST.INT.ARVL.)

1. Ask each student to research a country of their choice and draw a graph.

2. Put students in groups of four to combine their graphs and compare the figures.

3. Have students discuss the numbers and fluctuations and discuss what factors might cause the differences.

4. Give students 20 minutes to write up the findings following the model in Exercise 3.

Practice for the test (30 mins)

This can be done in class as pairwork or assigned for homework. Remind students to look back at the Exam tips in the unit. Point out that students can do more activities online if they want extra practice or to consolidate what they have learnt.

Task 1

Model answer
The line graph shows the percentage of tourists to Scotland who visited certain Edinburgh attractions between 1980 and 2010. We can see that in 1980 and in 2010 the favourite attractions were the castle and the festival. In 1980 the least popular attraction was the zoo but in 2010 this changed and the aquarium was the least popular.

During the 1980s and 1990s there was a rapid increase in visitors to the castle from 25% to 45%, and then the percentage gradually went down to 30% in 2010. The trend for the aquarium was similar to that for the castle. Visitors increased rapidly from 20% to 35% from 1980 to 1985 and then gradually decreased to less than 10% over the next 25 years. The number of tourists who visited the festival fluctuated slightly but in general remained stable at about 25%. Visitors to the zoo also fluctuated from 1980 to 2000 and then rose sharply from 10% to 20% between 2000 and 2010.

Listening: Completing forms

Student preparation for this class: Have students complete the Online / Workbook vocabulary preparation exercises at home before the lesson begins.

Teacher preparation: For the Spot check, create sets of cards for pelmanism (one set for each group of three students). On each card write one of the following words: *Australia, Australian, Egypt, Egyptian, Britain, British, Japan, Japanese, Pakistan, Pakistani, China, Chinese, Emirates, Emirati, Portugal, Portuguese, Malaysia, Malaysian, Spain, Spanish*. (25 mins)

Online / Workbook vocabulary preparation

Focus: The purpose of the exercises is to introduce country and nationality words; provide practice using words associated with flight information.

Develop your exam skills (Student's Book p. 91)

Focus: These exercises focus on Section 1 of the Listening test. They train students to listen for detailed information and to recognize number formats and spellings in order to complete forms.

Introduction
Use the Spot check to reinforce students' understanding of the Online / Workbook vocabulary preparation and revise country and nationality words.

Spot check
To reinforce country and nationality words, play pelmanism using words from Exercise 1 in the Workbook or Online.   **1.** Put students in groups of three and distribute sets of cards with country and nationality words.   **2.** Ask one member of each group to shuffle the cards and lay them face down on the table in a 4x5 grid.   **3.** Students take it in turns to turn two cards of their choice face up. If the cards match, e.g. *Britain* and *British*, they keep them. If the cards do not match, they put them face down again in their original positions.   **4.** Play continues until all the countries and nationalities have been matched. The student with the most pairs wins.

🎧 74 Exercise 1: Predicting and listening for numbers

a) Go over the Exam information on Section 1 of the Listening test. Draw students' attention to the first Exam tip. Remind them that the purpose of predicting is not so much to guess the right answers as to prepare to listen effectively. Refer students to the Grammar section: *Talking about future arrangements*.

b) Pair up students and give them a minute to make predictions.

c) Play the recording (track 74) and ask them to compare their answers.

> **Typical mistakes:** The prepositions *at* and *on* may be confusing to students because they can be used to refer to both time and place. The flight number may also be difficult to hear because it combines letters and numbers, and in particular numbers which sound similar, e.g. *fifteen* and *fifty*.

Answers
1 6.50 p.m.   **2** Wednesday 6th July   **3** British Airways / BA3025

🎧 75 Exercise 2: Identifying numbers

a) Before students listen, draw attention to the fact that numbers ending in -*teen* sound similar to numbers ending in -*ty*. Tell them to listen carefully to the recording (track 75) to hear which part of the word is spoken with most emphasis.

b) Do the exercise following the instructions in the book.

Answers
18 – eighteen; 13 – thirteen; 80 – eighty; 40 – forty;
15 – fifteen

 Exercise 3: Identifying numbers in sentences
Play the recording (track 76) once and let students compare answers in pairs. If there are any problems, play it a second time.

Answers
1 14 / fourteen **2** 40 / forty **3** 50 / fifty **4** 16.15 / sixteen fifteen **5** 17.30 / seventeen thirty

 Exercise 4: Spelling names correctly
a) Draw students' attention to the second Exam tip.

b) Ask students to do the exercise following the instructions in the book and compare their answers in groups of five.

c) To follow up, give students more practice writing names. Read and spell out selected names on your class register and challenge students to write them correctly.

> **Typical mistakes:** Depending on their first language, students may have difficulty distinguishing between *b, p* and *v; d* and *t; g* and *j;* and the vowels *a, e* and *i.*

Answers
1 b **2** c

 Exercise 5: Listening to complete a form
a) Pair students up and give them a minute to make predictions.

b) Play the recording (track 79) and ask them to compare their answers.

> **Typical mistakes:** Some students may note the time as 7.20 rather than 3.30 because 7.20 is the first time they hear. Refer them to the second Exam tip on page 92. If students have difficulty with the address, explain that in the UK, address components are normally given in the following order: house number, name of street, name of town, post code. If they have difficulty noting the post code, explain that UK postal codes normally consist of one or two letters followed by a number, then a number followed by one or two letters.

Answers
1 3.30 a.m. **2** 60 **3** ABINGDON **4** OX14 3HB
5 612744

 Exercise 6: Listening to complete a form
Students do the exercise following the instructions in the book and then compare their answers in pairs.

Answers
1 HUA FANG **2** 17 12 1994 **3** 13 PARK ROAD, BRIGHTON, BN40 4GR

Extension activity (20 mins)
To provide further practice in listening for information to complete a form, use the form in Exercise 6 as the basis for pairwork.

1. Explain to students that they are going to complete the form using information from their partner. Elicit questions for each item in the form, e.g. *What's your family name? Where were you born?*

2. Students pair up and ask each other the questions, noting the answers. Proper nouns should be spelt out. (Note: For item 3, students can give their real home address.)

 Practice for the test (20–30 mins)

This can be done in class as pairwork or assigned for homework. Remind students to look back at the Exam tips in the unit. Point out that students can do more activities online if they want extra practice or to consolidate what they have learnt.

Answers
1 Double – king-sized bed **2** Edward Francis **3** 23 Cypress **4** CB3 9NF **5** taxi **6** breakfast **7** Friday 16th April **8** c **9** b **10** c

Reading: Getting from place to place

> **Student preparation for this class:** Have students complete the Online / Workbook vocabulary preparation exercises at home before the lesson begins.
>
> **Teacher preparation:** Download and photocopy the Spot check 2 handout. Then cut out the sentences. Make one set of sentences for each group of students. If you don't want to download the handout, write the sentences on the board in advance. For the Extension activity, bring in a magazine article that will be of interest to your students and that states at least four strong opinions (that are not too difficult to follow). (15 mins)

Online / Workbook vocabulary preparation

> **Focus:** The purpose of the exercises is to introduce words relating to places and travel; extend travel phrases and focus on informal phrases; focus on distinguishing formal and informal language and genres.

Develop your exam skills (Student's Book p. 93)

> **Focus:** These exercises provide training in answering *Yes / No / Not Given* questions and help students identify the writer's opinion in a text.

Introduction

Use Spot check 1 to reinforce understanding of vocabulary connected with travel. Use Spot check 2 to help students practise identifying text types at the beginning or end of the lesson.

Spot check 1

To check the students' understanding of vocabulary connected with travel, do the following activity.

1. Put students in four teams. Give each team a category, but tell them that the category is secret. Suggested categories are as follows:
   Types of travel problem
   Ways of travelling
   Things that benefit travellers
   Types of road

2. Have each team look back at the blog in Exercise 3 in the Workbook / Online to find and list words and phrases that belong to their category. They can also add other words and phrases they know that fit in the category. Alternatively, simply ask them to think of words that belong to their category (without looking at the text).

3. Teams take it in turns to read out their lists and the other teams guess what the name of the category is.

Spot check 2

To give further practice in identifying text types, do the following activity.

1. Put students in groups of three and give them the sentences that you prepared before the lesson.

2. Students sort the sentences into three or four categories according to the text type.

3. Groups identify what sort of text each group of sentences comes from. (Possible answers: email or social networking post; formal letter; business report; newspaper article).

   Answers: email or social networking post: 1, 3, 7; formal letter: 2, 6, 8; news article: 4, 5, 9

Exercise 1: Distinguishing between facts and opinions

a) Go over the Exam information on *Yes / No / Not Given* questions. Check that students understand the difference between these questions and *True / False / Not Given* questions that are about information rather than opinion.

b) Exercise 1 encourages students to look at the language of factual and opinion statements. Ask students to do the exercise individually following the instructions in the book and compare their answers in groups.

c) Follow up by asking them what features of sentences 4 and 7 helped them decide that they were opinions.

Typical mistakes: Students may mistake opinions for facts unless the writer uses strong opinion language to introduce their opinion. It can be helpful to look at individual words and phrases that indicate opinion language, such as evaluative adjectives and adverbs, e.g. *good, well, harmful, badly,* and hedging language and modals, e.g. *may, possibly, surely, should*.

Answers
1 F 2 F 3 F 4 O 5 F 6 F 7 O

Exercise 2: Identifying whether a writer agrees or disagrees with an opinion

Have students read the instructions carefully. They should identify the opinions for each text individually and then compare answers in pairs before moving on to the next text.

Answers
Text 1
1 NO 2 YES 3 YES 4 YES
Text 2
5 NO 6 NO 7 YES
Text 3
8 YES 9 YES 10 YES 11 NO 12 YES

Exercise 3: Identifying synonyms and paraphrases

a) Draw attention to the Exam tip before you move on to the exercise.

b) Students should underline the key words in the text before checking with their partner. They then compare their answers with the ones in the key.

Answers
Text 1
1 ... Do people using transport feel reassured ...? Possibly. But most of them, especially visitors to the UK, may feel that there is something to worry about ...
2 ... the police, armed or not, cannot protect us from bombers.
3 But what the police can, and sometimes do do, is make mistakes, and these are always worse when there are firearms involved.
4 So in the end, arming police may do more harm than good.

Text 2
5 Instead of complaining about roadworks ...
6 I say we try to save our environment by ...
7 I say we try ... by campaigning for better bus and train networks and ... trams.

Text 3
8 The rise in fuel prices is a very worrying trend.
9 Here are ... examples of the consequences.
10 ... prices of ... food ... also increase as a direct result of the cost of oil, e.g. ... beef
11 ... there is one possible advantage ... But surely, this is not enough.
12 What we need is ... to reduce fuel prices and/or financially support those who are being affected.

Exercise 4: Identifying opinions in texts

Students do the exercise and then check answers in groups, referring back to the language in the text that helped them choose their answers.

Answers

1 NOT GIVEN   2 ✓   3 ✓   4 NOT GIVEN
5 ✓   6 NOT GIVEN

Extension activity (40 mins)

To provide further practice in locating opinions in a text, have students read the text you sourced and brought to class.

1. Put students in groups of three and have them write down eight sentences on a piece of paper: four sentences that paraphrase opinions from the text and four sentences that give opinions that are NOT in the text.

2. Have groups swap sentences and find and tick the four sentences that match the opinions stated in the text.

Practice for the test (30 mins)

This can be done in class as pairwork or assigned for homework. Remind students to look back at the Exam tips in the unit. Point out that students can do more activities online if they want extra practice or to consolidate what they have learnt.

Answers

1 YES   **2** NOT GIVEN   **3** YES   **4** NOT GIVEN
5 NOT GIVEN   **6** YES   **7** NO   **8** YES   **9** NO
10 NOT GIVEN   **11** NOT GIVEN   **12** YES

UNIT 10: HEALTH

Listening: Food and nutrition

Student preparation for this class: Have students complete the Online / Workbook vocabulary preparation exercises at home before the lesson begins.

Teacher preparation: For Spot check 1, make sets of cards with the words in Exercises 1 and 2 in the Workbook or Online. Write one word per card and make sufficient sets for each groups of four students. (25 mins)

Online / Workbook vocabulary preparation

Focus: The purpose of these exercises is to introduce vocabulary relating to food and cooking; introduce words for weights and measures.

Develop your exam skills (Student's Book p. 96)

Focus: These exercises focus on Section 2 of the Listening test. They train students to identify stages in a process. Exercises 4 and 5 provide practice in completing flow charts and notes, keeping to the specified word limit.

Introduction

1   Introduce the unit by getting students to talk about the pictures on pages 104 and 105 in pairs. Ask them to talk about what they can see and how it relates to the unit topic, Health. Elicit ideas and opinions about what students do or should do to keep healthy.

2   Use Spot check 1 to reinforce students' understanding of the Online / Workbook vocabulary preparation and revise food vocabulary. You can use the Spot check 2 after Exercise 1 or at another appropriate time during the lesson.

Spot check

To check food-related vocabulary, have students talk about the foods they like and dislike.

1.   Pre-teach a selection of sentence stems for expressing likes and dislikes: *I love …, I (quite) like …, I'm not too keen on …, I dislike/don't like …, I can't stand …*

2.   Put students in groups of four and designate one person in each group the facilitator. Place face down one set of cards with words from Exercises 1 and 2 in front of each group.

3.   Students take it in turns to pick a card and say whether they like or dislike the food. If the food is countable, they should refer to it in the plural form, e.g. *I like beans.* If it is uncountable, they should use the singular, e.g. *I like lamb.*

4.   Facilitators use the answer key to monitor correct use of countable and uncountable nouns.

5.   To make the exercise more challenging, ask students to incorporate the cooking words in Exercise 3 in the Workbook or Online to form sentences,
e.g. *I dislike boiled carrots. I like fried eggs.*

Spot check 2

To reinforce students' comprehension of fractions, dictate a selection of fractions, e.g. *nine tenths, two thirds, five sixths*. Students listen and write what they hear in numerical form, e.g. $^9/_{10}$, $^2/_3$, $^5/_6$.

 Exercise 1: Listening for quantities and measurements
a)   Go over the Exam information on Section 2 of the Listening test on page 96.

b)   Give students a few minutes to think of alternative ways of expressing the quantities a–h and to predict which quantities are likely to go with which ingredients.

c)   Play the recording twice (track 83) and check answers.

> **Typical mistakes:** If students confuse 15 ml and 50 ml, remind them of the stress patterns: 15 = weak-strong; 50 = strong-weak.

Answers
2 c   3 d   4 a   5 h   6 g

 Exercise 2: Ordering stages of a process
a)   Have students work in pairs to predict the correct order of the photos and anticipate vocabulary they are likely to hear. Check their understanding of cooking-related verbs by miming *weigh, mix, pour* and *flip* and asking students to identify the correct verb.

b)   Play the recording (track 84) and have students check their answers.

c)   To reinforce awareness of sequencing words, play the recording again and ask students to raise their hands every time they hear a word or expression such as *when, next, then, at that point*.

Answers
D, E, A, G, F, C, B

 Exercise 3: Completing a flow chart
a)   Give students time to look at the flow chart and predict the vocabulary and type of information they are likely to hear in pairs.

b)   Play the recording (track 85) and have them complete the exercise.

Answers

1 slice the apples   **2** (apples) with sugar   **3** blackberries and apples   **4** (a) baking dish   **5** flour and butter (together)   **6** (the) sugar   **7** on top / on top of fruit
8 30 minutes

 Exercise 4: Completing notes

a)   Spend 2–3 minutes talking about what students already know about traditional English meals. Pair students up and give them a minute to make predictions.

b)   Play the recording (track 86) and ask them to compare their answers.

Answers

1 deep fat   **2** healthy   **3** Friday night   **4** roast
5 vegetables   **6** at home

Extension activity (20–30 mins)

To provide further practice in listening to process descriptions and completing flow charts, pair students up to exchange recipes.

1.   Give students a few minutes to think of a regional dish and how it is prepared.

2.   Have each student describe the process while their partner listens and notes the information in the form of a flow chart.

3.   Students who are unable to describe a recipe can talk about a few traditional meals while their partner takes notes.

 Practice for the test (30 mins)

This can be done in class as pairwork or assigned for homework. Remind students to look back at the Exam tips in the unit. Point out that students can do more activities online if they want extra practice or to consolidate what they have learnt.

Answers

1 eat properly   **2** improving situation   **3** right amount
4 dairy foods   **5–7** (in any order) a, b, g   **8** government
9 schools   **10** families / parents

Speaking: Sport and exercise

Student preparation for this class: Have students complete the Online / Workbook language preparation exercises at home before the lesson begins.

Teacher preparation: None

Online / Workbook language preparation

Focus: These exercises introduce language for talking about health: introducing words and phrases associated with healthy activities; focusing on language to give explanations; focusing on the pronunciation of contractions; focusing on grammar: *should* and *shouldn't*.

Develop your exam skills (Student's Book p. 98)

Focus: These exercises focus on Parts 1 and 3 of the Speaking test: Exercises 1–2 focus on giving relevant information and opinions when answering questions in Part 1; Exercises 3–7 focus on identifying question types in Part 3.

Introduction

Use Spot check 1 to reinforce students' understanding of the Online / Workbook language preparation and review collocations with *do* and *play*. You can use Spot check 2 to review advice language before doing Exercises 3–7, or at another appropriate stage of the lesson.

Spot check 1

To check students' recall of vocabulary for describing healthy activities, do the following activity.

1.   Ask students to close their books. Put them in groups of 3–4. Put the following table on the board:

do	play

2.   Students write down as many healthy activities you can 'do' or 'play' as they can in two minutes. They receive two points if the word or phrase was mentioned in Unit 10 and one point for any other words or phrases they have found. They lose a point for anything that is not in the correct column or that is not a healthy activity.

3.   When the two minutes are up, look at the lists (to avoid cheating). Ask the teams to take it in turns to read out one of their words. Write the words on the board and give the teams points. Congratulate the winning team at the end.

The following words and phrases will score two points each:

do	play
yoga	*table tennis*
tae kwon do	*brain training games*
	board games
	sports
	a musical instrument
	chess

Spot check 2

To check students' ability to use vocabulary for giving explanations, to use *should and shouldn't*, and to practise the pronunciation of contractions, do the following activity.

1. Ask students to stay in the same groups as for Spot check 1. Tell them they have another chance to win.

2. Write the following on the board:

   a) *People should play … . It's a … idea because it keeps their mind … .*
   b) *It's important to stay … . Doing … can help but people … do too much of it when they start.*
   c) *It's quite … when you first start an activity but you … keep going. After all the hard work, you'll feel more … .*

3. Students complete the gaps with suitable words. The first group to complete the gaps correctly wins.

4. Groups take it in turns to read out one of their answers. There is at least one contraction in each answer, so check that these are pronounced correctly.

Note: the following are some possible answers, but accept any others that make sense.

   a) board games / chess, good / great, active / busy

   b) healthy / fit / active, sports / yoga, shouldn't

   c) challenging / difficult, should, relaxed / healthy

Exercise 1: Choosing appropriate answers to Part 1 questions

a) Go over the Exam information.

b) Have students do Exercise 1 in pairs and then check answers. Ask learners to explain why there is a problem with the incorrect answer.

> **Typical mistakes:** Students are often nervous at the start of the Speaking test and are happy when they hear a question they understand. This can lead to giving an answer too quickly and it may not be completely relevant.

Answers
1 a 2 a 3 a 4 b

Exercise 2: Checking answers for relevance

a) Draw attention to the first Exam tip.

b) Tell students to make sure they understand the whole question. For example, in Exercise 1, question 3, they need to give an answer to the question *When?* and talk about seeing both friends and family. Encourage them to repeat the question they hear in their heads, and to think about all the aspects before giving an answer. Phrases they have already learnt, such as *Let me see,* can give them time to think.

c) If possible, record students' answers to the questions in Exercise 1 and/or have them work in pairs and give feedback on each other's answers.

 ## Exercise 3: Identifying what Part 3 questions are asking for

a) Draw students' attention to the second Exam tip.

b) Have them listen to the recording (track 90) and note down their answers before checking them in pairs.

Answers
a 2 b 1 c 3

 ## Exercise 4: Identifying useful language in Part 3 answers

a) Ask students to read the answers and underline the phrases individually before comparing their ideas in pairs or groups.

b) Then play the recording (track 91) to focus on how each phrase is pronounced.

Answers
a I think …, in my opinion, …, I think …
b We should …, they could …, We should …
c I think …, you can …

Exercise 5: Analysing Part 3 answers

Have students read the model answers again and follow the instructions for the exercise. They should compare their answers in pairs.

Answers
1 Answer a: yes; Answer b: yes; Answer c: no – The student talks about different sports and sports he would like to do.
2 Answer a: opinion – important to slow down and relax; Answer b: suggestion – encourage young people to play outdoors and learn about food; Answer c: comparison – not made

 ## Exercise 6: Giving answers to Part 3 questions

a) Ask students to think about the questions and make notes to plan their answers if necessary. Refer to the Grammar section: *Should, ought to.*

b) Have them record themselves if possible and then listen to each other's answers and assess them.

 ## Exercise 7: Analysing Part 3 questions and giving relevant answers

a) Play the recording (track 92). Students discuss in pairs or groups what the question is asking for.

b) They should give their answers without writing anything down. Have students listen to a partner's answers and give feedback on whether their answers were relevant or not.

> **Typical mistakes:** Students may give an answer without thinking what a questions is actually asking for. If you notice that this happens a lot, draw their attention to the answers in Exercise 4. There is a pattern: an immediate response (*Definitely / That's a difficult question / That's interesting*), which may

include a phrase to get some time to think (*That's interesting / Let me see*), and then the actual answer with an explanation, examples and conclusions.

Answers
1 opinion   2 suggestion   3 comparison

Extension activity (15 mins)
To provide further speaking opportunities and to practise using a range of vocabulary about a topic, do the following activity.

1. Give students some time to write down three questions asking for someone's opinion about healthy living, e.g. *In your opinion, is yoga a sport? Do you think there should be a maximum number of junk food restaurants in any local area?*

2. Have students walk around and ask three different people one of their questions.

3. After they have answered, they can give feedback to each other about the answers (on relevance, length of answer and use of vocabulary).

Practice for the test (30 mins)

This can be done in class as pairwork or assigned for homework. Remind students to look back at the Exam tips in the unit. Point out that students can do more activities online if they want extra practice or to consolidate what they have learnt.

Part 1
Exercise 1
Model answers
1 I like doing sports. My favourite sport is tennis. I enjoy playing tennis outdoors when it's hot.
2 It depends. Sometimes I watch important football games on TV. I prefer listening to sports on the radio or on my mobile.
3 Yes, I like playing golf. I always play at the weekend with my friends. I often go to the gym too. It's important to keep fit.
4 In my country, the most popular sport is football. Everybody loves it. Young boys play football every day and they'd like to be professional football players.
5 I spend four or five hours a week on my hobbies. I'd like to spend more time on my hobbies and interests, but my university course is very hard.

Part 2
Exercise 2
Model answer
I'd like to describe an activity I like doing to keep healthy. This activity is yoga.

I really enjoy doing yoga. I do yoga every week and I do it in two different places. Firstly, I do yoga in my bedroom. Sometimes I do it after a hard day at university, but I usually do it in the morning. Secondly, I do yoga at a yoga centre near university.

In my opinion, it keeps me healthy in different ways. It's good for my body because I have to be strong and fit. It's really challenging! It's good for my mind too, because I have to focus on one thing. It's good to forget about studying and exams when you're tired.

Finally, I like doing it because it's important to keep fit and it makes me feel very relaxed and calm. I don't like going to gyms or noisy places, so doing yoga at home or in a quiet class is great.

Exercise 3
Model answers
1 No, they don't. My sister likes doing tae kwon do. She tried yoga but she didn't like it. My brother prefers playing football or cricket. He likes team sports.
2 Yes, I'd like to do yoga every day. I'm going to do more yoga after my exams finish. In fact, I'm going on a yoga holiday in the summer.

Part 3
Exercise 4
Model answers
1 That's an interesting question. There are lots of differences between sports now and in the past. I think money is one big difference. For example, big companies sponsor some sports competitions and competitors can win lots of money. Technology is another difference. For example, motor racing is different compared to the past. Today the cars are very fast and drivers often make new records.

2 I'm not sure. I think some people eat better because they have lots of money. They can buy different kinds of fresh food or they can go to the best restaurants. Cooking is a popular hobby for some people. But there are lots of poor people in my country and they don't eat well. For example, they have to eat cheap food or junk food and this is bad for them.

3 That's interesting. Firstly, I think we should encourage young people to be healthy because health is important. We should use the media and famous people to encourage young people. For example, TV shows can show people doing exciting sports. Famous people can describe activities or healthy diets. Finally, parents should show their children how to be healthy.

4 Yes, definitely. In my opinion, I think the government should teach people about healthy lifestyles. For example, they could give people information about healthy diets so they can eat well. They should describe different activities that are good for your mind and for your body. Then people can be fit, happy and healthy.

Reading: Body and mind

Student preparation for this class: Have students complete the Online / Workbook vocabulary preparation exercises at home before the lesson begins.

Teacher preparation: For Spot check 2, prepare sets of cards with words in Exercise 4 in the Workbook / Online (one word per card). Make one set for each group of four students. For the Extension activity, source and photocopy two health-related texts of an appropriate level of difficulty (300–400 words each). (30 mins)

Online / Workbook vocabulary preparation

Focus: The purpose of these exercises is to introduce words related to sports; introduce words for describing feelings; focus on adjectives ending in -ed and -ing.

Develop your exam skills (Student's Book p. 100)

Focus: These exercises train students to answer short-answer questions and keep to word limits.

Introduction

Use Spot checks 1 and 2 to reinforce students' understanding of the Online / Workbook vocabulary preparation and revise sport vocabulary and vocabulary for feelings.

Spot check 1

To reinforce vocabulary relating to sport, do the following activity.

1. Put students in groups of four.
2. Have students take it in turns to choose one of the sports in Exercise 3 and, without saying what the sport is, describe it to the other group members, e.g. *Two or four people can play this sport. You can play it inside or outside. You need a ball and rackets.* (Answer: tennis)
3. Listeners try to guess the sport being described.

Spot check 2

To reinforce vocabulary for describing feelings, play the following game.

1. Give students one minute to revise the words in Exercise 4 in the Workbook or Online.
2. Put students in teams of four.
3. In front of each team place face down a set of cards with words from Exercise 4.
4. The members of the team take it in turns to pick the top card and mime the feeling for the other members of the team to guess.
5. The team that correctly guesses the most words in 10 minutes wins.

Exercise 1: Keeping to the word limit

a) Go over the Exam information on short-answer questions on page 100. Give students a few minutes to discuss what they find difficult about short-answer questions and the strategies they use to answer them.

b) Draw students' attention to the Exam tip. Then have students do the exercise individually and compare their answers in pairs.

Suggested answers
2 during pregnancy   **3** he needs medication
4 (no change necessary)

Exercise 2: Writing short answers using word limits

a) Ask students to do the exercise individually and compare their answers in groups of three or four.

b) Follow up by asking each pair to write a question for another pair to answer in no more than three words.

Typical mistakes: Students who have difficulty expressing themselves within the word limit can be encouraged to focus on key content words, especially nouns, verbs, adjectives and adverbs.

Possible answers
1 regular exercise (2 words)   **2** I love it (3 words)
3 reading, watching films (3 words)   **4** to keep fit (3 words)

Exercise 3: Tips for answering short-answer questions

a) Explain the importance of using the most appropriate reading strategies for the task in the Reading test. Then have students read the questions before they look at the reading tips.

b) Have them do the exercise in small groups and follow up with whole class feedback. Encourage students to explain their choice of answers.

Typical mistakes: Students who are very text-focused rather than task-focused may need to be persuaded of the utility of strategies such as scanning. Explain that the kind of reading they need to do for the exam is more like reading for 'research', i.e. reading to find answers to questions, than reading a text book, which typically involves comprehensive learning of information.

Answer
The following wouldn't help: reading the text before reading the questions; underlining the key words in the text.

Exercise 4: Answering short-answer questions

a) Students work individually to underline the key words in the questions and then write their answers.

b) They should compare their answers in pairs. Reasonable alternative responses are acceptable, e.g. *definitions of health* for *health definitions* or *manage everyday tasks* for *ability to cope.*

Suggested answers

1 they are older   **2** health definitions   **3** ability to cope

Extension activity (40 mins)

To provide further practice in answering short-answer questions, have students write exam questions for each other.

1. Put students in two groups. Hand out one of the texts you have sourced to one group and the other text to the other group.

2. Have students read their text carefully, and in pairs or small groups write five short-answer questions along with answers of no more than three words each. Circulate as they work, checking for accuracy.

3. Have students from different groups swap reading texts and questions. See which group can correctly answer all five questions the fastest.

Practice for the test (30 mins)

This can be done in class as pairwork or assigned for homework. Remind students to look back at the Exam tips in the unit. Point out that students can do more activities online if they want extra practice or to consolidate what they have learnt.

Suggested answers

1 shapes, heights, colours, abilities   **2** genetics, ageing, social factors   **3** physically difficult or inactive
4 housing (conditions) and neighbourhoods   **5** culture and media   **6** the idea of slimness / ideal body shape
7 belly or stomach   **8** biologically and socially
9 exercise and food   **10** wrong and unhealthy

Writing: Healthcare and lifestyle

> **Student preparation for this class:** Have students complete the Online / Workbook language preparation exercises at home before the lesson begins.
>
> **Teacher preparation:** None

Online / Workbook language preparation

> **Focus:** The purpose of these exercises is to introduce words associated with health; introduce the first and second conditionals.

Develop your exam skills (Student's Book p. 103)

> **Focus:** These exercises train students to write about cause and effect using conditional sentences and appropriate linking words in preparation for one of the question types in Task 2.

Introduction

Use Spot check 1 to revise health vocabulary and practise using conditional structures from the Online / Workbook vocabulary preparation.

Spot check

To check students' recall of words associated with health and to practise the first and second conditionals, organize a role play to discuss how to deal with the problem of obesity.

1. Allocate the following two types of roles: doctors/admin and nurses/support staff. Have doctors and admin use the first conditional to express more certain views, and the nurses and support staff use the second conditional to express more tentative views.

2. Have students prepare their roles by thinking of how they can use the words from Exercises 1 and 2 in the Workbook or Online in conditional sentences to express their own views on what to do about the problem of obesity. Ask them to think of at least three sentences.

3. Tell students to try to use their conditional sentences in a natural context without the others noticing. Award points for each use of a conditional that goes unnoticed. When the discussion is complete, have students swap roles and discuss another topic such as the advantages and disadvantages of free healthcare.

Note: You might find you need to act as chairperson, but if so, use this role to encourage discussion rather than an opportunity to give your own views.

Exercise 1: Identifying cause and effect sentences

a) Go through the Exam information on page 103. Ask questions, e.g.

   What language do you use to describe cause and effect?

   Can you give an example of a linking word that introduces an effect?

   Draw attention to the Exam tip and refer to the Grammar section: *Talking about cause and effect.*

b) Have students do Exercise 1 individually and compare their answers in pairs.

c) You will notice that there is one other sentence in the paragraph indicating cause and effect, and one more indicating effect only; students may have underlined these. They are:

   The cost of healthcare (C) *should not stop people going to the doctor.* (E)

   The result of this could be an unequal and divided society. (E)

The reason the first sentence is not included in the answer key is because it does not follow the conditional pattern highlighted in this section, but it is worth noting. The second sentence only expresses effect so is not included in the answer key. However, it does include one of the linking phrases referred to in the Exam information box and is also worth noting.

Answer

There is also a second important issue to take into account. (C) If poor people have to pay for healthcare, (E) they might not visit the doctor when they are ill. (C) If healthcare becomes more expensive, (E) <u>there may be some negative effects in the future</u>. For example, (C) <u>if only rich people can afford healthcare</u>, (E) <u>they may be much healthier and may live longer than poor people</u>. The result of this could be an unequal and divided society.

Exercise 2: Using conditional structures to express cause and effect

Have students complete the exercise individually and check their answers in pairs or small groups.

> **Typical mistakes:** It is common for students to make mistakes with the structure of conditionals despite teacher input. It is, therefore, useful to have some exercises that force them to pay attention to accuracy.

Answers

1 free healthcare might not do them much good
2 if people have unhealthy lifestyles
3 they should pay for it themselves

Exercise 3: Completing cause and effect sentences

a) Highlight the different ways that cause and effect sentences can be structured. Point out that students should vary the pattern in their writing to maintain interest.

b) Students do the exercise individually and check their answers in pairs.

Answers

2 Because young children spend too much time watching television (C), they do not get enough exercise (E).
3 Many people have office jobs which do not involve any physical activity (C). As a result, they aren't active enough (E).
4 Because their parents do not teach them (C), children do not know how to cook for themselves (E).
5 Due to the availability of cheap fast food (C), people do not shop for fresh food (E).
6 Governments earn a lot of money from fast food companies (E) because they tax them heavily (C).

Exercise 4: Correcting mistakes with linking words

a) In this exercise students have to use their editing skills. Prompt them to find the mistakes for themselves rather than giving them the answers. For example, if they can't identify the first mistake, ask them to list the linking words that express effect.

b) Encourage students to discuss their answers in pairs or small groups.

Answers

... people don't get enough exercise ~~due to~~ *because* they have jobs ... make their own bread. ~~Result~~ *As a result*, they were more active in their lives. ... have cars in the old days, ~~because~~ *so* they had to walk everywhere. ... Now, ~~due~~ *due to* cars and machines .... ~~In result~~ *As a result*, they become more unfit.

Exercise 5: Matching cause and effect clauses

a) Have students read the sentences carefully before they match them.

b) Have whole class feedback and elicit ideas for suitable ways to link each cause and effect.

Answers

1 c **2** e **3** d **4** a **5** b

Exercise 6: Writing a paragraph explaining causes and effects

Have students write the paragraph and then compare what they have written in pairs. During feedback, briefly discuss whether they agreed with their partner's arguments.

Model answer

Many health problems today may be caused by modern technology. For example, if children spend too much time playing video games, they may not do enough exercise and may become overweight. Also, people who use computers at work can develop health problems, such as wrist problems or back pain, because they spend all day sitting in the same position. Finally, people spend less time playing healthy sports because they prefer to use social media.

Extension activity (50 mins)

Have students work in groups to discuss the texts in Exercises 1, 2 and 4. Have them identify where they disagree with the writer, noting their own views. They then rewrite the texts to express their own views.

Practice for the test (40 mins)

This can be done in class as pairwork or assigned for homework. Remind students to look back at the Exam tips in the unit. Point out that students can do more activities online if they want extra practice or to consolidate what they have learnt.

Task 2

Model answer

Healthcare is very important for everyone in the world but it can be very expensive. Many people believe that governments should try to prevent illness by making sure everyone in their country has a healthy lifestyle. I agree that preventing illness is better than curing it.

The cost of medical treatment can be high so governments have to think of ways to encourage people to be healthier. If people are healthy, they will not need medical care so often. Many diseases can be prevented if people have good diets, take exercise and give up unhealthy habits such as smoking. If people cannot work or care for themselves or their family due to illness, this will cost governments and taxpayers a lot of money. In my opinion, governments should spend money on producing information leaflets and films that encourage people to follow healthy lifestyles, such as eating plenty of fruit and vegetables, taking regular exercise and giving up smoking. Governments should also try to reduce environmental pollution because this can cause illness and health problems.

However, having a healthy lifestyle cannot prevent all health problems. There are many diseases, such as cancer, that are a result of living in the modern world and that cannot be prevented by a healthy lifestyle. Accidents at work or on the roads will also cause injuries that need medical treatment. If governments focus mainly on prevention, there may be less money for urgent healthcare and many people could suffer.

In conclusion, I believe that governments should provide a balance of prevention and treatment because of the different types of health problem, but their main focus should be on prevention rather than cure.

UNIT 11: TAKING RESPONSIBILITY

Reading: Rights and responsibilities

Student preparation for this class: Have students complete the Online / Workbook language preparation exercises at home before the lesson begins.

Teacher preparation: Download and photocopy the Spot check 1 handout. Cut up both the words *(chairperson, secretary, student representative, teaching staff, committee member, head teacher)* and the corresponding blank cards. You will need one set for each group of four students. You will also need strips of paper (long enough to write sentences on) for the Extension activity. Prepare six strips for each pair of students. (15 mins)

Online / Workbook language preparation

Focus: The purpose of these exercises is to introduce words relating to professional meetings and responsibilities; focus on sentence structure and subjects that have more than one noun.

Develop your exam skills (Student's Book p. 106)

Focus: These exercises train students to do multiple-choice questions by choosing the correct sentence endings.

Introduction

1   Introduce the unit by getting students to talk about the pictures on pages 109, 110 and 111 in pairs. Ask them to see if they can identify any links between the photos and decide how they relate to the unit topic, *Taking responsibility*. Elicit which picture is linked to the Reading section topic of young people's rights and responsibilities. Recycle some of the job vocabulary from the Online / Workbook language preparation.

2   Use Spot check 1 to recycle vocabulary relating to groups and meetings from the Online / Workbook language preparation. Use Spot check 2 at an appropriate stage of the lesson to review sentences with complex subjects.

Spot check 1

To reinforce vocabulary relating to professional meetings and groups, do the following activity.

1.   Give students one minute to revise the words in Exercise 1 of the Workbook or Online.

2.   Put students in groups of four and give each group a set of the cards you prepared before the class (six cards with words and six blank cards).

3.   The group discuss what they think each role involves and write a definition for it on one of the blank cards, e.g. *This person belongs to a*

group with special responsibilities at a meeting (committee member).

4.   Each group shuffles their cards and swaps cards with another group.

5.   Students match the people to the definitions that the other group wrote.

6.   Groups discuss whether the definitions on the other group's cards are similar to the definitions they wrote themselves. Ask them if they can think of any other roles or responsibilities that students and teachers might have at a school, e.g. *mentor, head boy/girl, deputy head*.

Spot check 2

To check the students' understanding of sentences with long or complex subjects, do the following activity.

1.   Put students in two or three teams, depending on the size of the class. Choose one of the sentences from Exercise 4 and write it on the board.

2.   Teams should take turns to delete 1–3 words of the sentence, ensuring that it still makes sense and is grammatically correct. They score a point for each word they delete. For example:

The secret of a successful career, according to my mother, is to have children first, when you are still young.

Team 1: *The secret of a successful career, according to my mother, is to have children ~~first~~ when you are ~~still~~ young.* (2 points)

Team 2: *The secret of a successful career, according to my mother, is to have children ~~when you are~~ young.* (3 points)

Team 1: *The secret of a successful career, according to ~~my~~ mother, is: to have children young.* (2 points)

Team 2: *The secret of a successful career ~~according to mother~~ is: have children young.* (3 points)

Exercise 1: Predicting sentence endings

a)   Go over the Exam information on matching sentence endings and have a short discussion on how students feel about these types of questions. Draw attention to the first Exam tip on page 106 and point out that Exercise 1 will help students to do this.

b)   Before students do the exercise, check understanding of the word *charter* by explaining or giving some examples of different charters, e.g. *government charter, human rights charter, school charter*.

c)   Ask students to cover Exercise 2 and do Exercise 1, following the instructions in the book and then compare their answers in groups.

Possible answers

1 The African Charter on the rights and welfare of the … – (adjective +) noun, e.g. (*African*) *people*
2 The name was chosen … – preposition, e.g. *by* …; verb, e.g. *to help*
3 This Children's Charter … – verb, e.g. *has*; relative pronoun, e.g. *which*
4 It covers the economic, social, political and cultural … – noun, e.g. *issues*
5 Education needs to be … – verb, adverb, adjective, e.g. *encouraged / efficiently / good*

Exercise 2: Matching sentence beginnings and endings

a) Draw students' attention to the second Exam tip on page 106. Ask students to do the exercise individually and compare their answers in pairs.

b) Get feedback on whether the answers were similar to their ideas in Exercise 1. Follow up by asking them what features of the answers helped them decide on their answers, e.g. an adjective precedes a noun.

Answers
a 2   **b** 1   **c** 4   **d** 3

Exercise 3: Choosing sentence endings

a) Exercise 3 involves looking closely at the information in the text as well as the grammar of the sentence endings. Have students do the exercise individually, following the instructions in the book.

b) As you check student's answers, challenge them to explain why the other answers were incorrect. This will help them recognize typical features of distractors (wrong answers).

Answers
1 c   **2** c   **3** b   **4** b   **5** c

Extension activity (30 mins)

To provide further practice in choosing correct sentence endings, have pairs of students write sentence halves for another pair to match.

1. It would be useful to demonstrate the activity by writing a sentence on the board and then splitting it into two suitable segments, e.g. *One of the most basic human rights is / to have clean drinking water*.

2. Have students work in pairs. Give each pair six strips of paper. They read the text in Exercise 3 on page 107 again and decide on six sentences of at least eight words to write on the strips of paper (one sentence per strip).

3. They then cut each sentence into two parts and swap strips with another pair.

4. Pairs look at the sentence beginnings they have been given and guess the likely endings (without looking back at the text).

5. Pairs look at the sentence endings and match them to the correct beginnings.

Practice for the test (30 mins)

This can be done in class as pairwork or assigned for homework. Remind students to look back at the Exam tips in the unit. Point out that students can do more activities online if they want extra practice or to consolidate what they have learnt.

Answers
1 G (see introductory paragraph)
2 H ('dress code' refers to 'uniform')
3 E (see point 1 under 'Year councils')
4 D (see point 7 under 'Year councils')
5 C (see last paragraph)

Writing: Making choices

Student preparation for this class: Have students complete the Online / Workbook language preparation exercises at home before the lesson begins.

Teacher preparation: For Spot check 1, prepare large cards, each with one of the eight words from Exercise 1 in the Workbook or Online + additional known transport words. For Spot check 2, download and photocopy the handout (one per student). (15 mins)

Online / Workbook language preparation

Focus: The purpose of these exercises is to introduce words associated with transport; introduce verbs followed by *to* + infinitive or the *-ing* form; introduce the zero article / plurals to talk about things in general.

Develop your exam skills (Student's Book p. 109)

Focus: These exercises train students to write problem and solution essays in preparation for one of the question types in Task 2.

Introduction

Use Spot check 1 to recycle vocabulary connected with transport and reinforce the Online / Workbook language preparation. Use Spot check 2 to focus on gerunds and infinitives at an appropriate point in the lesson.

Spot check 1
To check students' recall of words associated with transport, do a mingling activity. 1. Pin one of the cards you have prepared on each of the students' backs without letting them see what it is. If you have more than eight students, make more cards with other suitable words such as *underground* and *airport* so there are enough for each student. 2. Have students mingle and ask each other questions to find out the word on their back. They can only ask *Yes / No* questions, e.g. *Is it a problem?* However, they must not ask directly

about the word, e.g. *Is it pollution?* Of course, once they are sure, they say what they think the word is.

3. When they have all found their words, ask each student to say something personal about transport – an opinion or an experience – using their word.

If students are finding this activity difficult, write the words on the board so that they know what words they can choose from. However, it is best to challenge students first and let them try to do the activity without the words on the board.

As an extension to this activity, add a few more general words about transport to the board, e.g. *trains, public transport, flights*. Then ask students to talk about transport in general. Listen and check that they are using the correct articles, zero article, plurals, etc.

Spot check 2

To check students' understanding of verb + *-ing* / infinitive with *to*, have them complete statements about themselves using the Spot check 2 handout. Ask them to use verbs in their answers. When they have completed the exercise, they can ask and answer questions in pairs, e.g.

S1: *What do you want to do before your next birthday?*

S2: *I want to buy a new car. Why did you decide to take the IELTS exam?*

Exercise 1: Identifying sentences that state problems and propose solutions

a) Go through the Exam information on page 109. Ask questions, e.g.

What do you explain first, the problem or the solution?

How many solutions do you need to think of?

How many ways can you structure these essays?

b) Have students do Exercise 1 individually and then compare their answers in pairs.

Answers
1 S   2 S   3 P   4 S   5 P   6 P   7 P   8 S

Exercise 2: Matching problems to proposed solutions

Have students complete the exercise individually and then check their answers in pairs or small groups. During feedback, encourage students to evaluate the suggested solutions.

Typical mistakes: Students can sometimes find it difficult to think of solutions to problems. Encourage them to see solutions as possibilities that may or may not be effective. The important thing when writing is to come up with ideas, even if the ideas are not very good.

Answers
1 c   2 b   3 d   4 a

Exercise 3: Ordering notes for a structure 1 problem and solution essay

a) Check that students understand the pattern of a **structure 1 problem and solution essay** (problem – solution, problem – solution). Refer to the Grammar section: *Should, ought to.*

b) Have students do the exercise individually and then check answers in pairs.

c) Draw attention to the Exam tip and encourage students to use a clear structure when writing their own notes.

Suggested answers
(The order of paragraphs here is the correct order for a structure 1 problem and solution essay.)
A Paragraph 2: Introduction
B Paragraph 3: Problem 1 + solutions
C Paragraph 1: Problem 2 + solutions
D Paragraph 4: Conclusion

Exercise 4: Expanding notes into a full essay

a) This is an opportunity for students to concentrate on accuracy as they have already been given the ideas and vocabulary to use. Give students enough time to think about what they are writing.

b) Monitor as they write their essays.

c) Encourage discussion in pairs when they have finished writing. Identify the structure of the essay during feedback (problem – solution, problem – solution).

Model answer
Public transport is essential for going to and from work and school. However it can be expensive and crowded. In my opinion, it needs better planning. This essay will describe the problems involved in public transport and suggest possible solutions.

Firstly, there is a problem with the cost of public transport. Fares can be very high and so people do not use it and drive cars instead. As a result, the number of cars on the roads is increasing. In my opinion, fares should be reduced for some people, such as old people and students. Many people also think that driving should be made more expensive. For example, cars could be taxed more and parking could be more expensive. This will make public transport cheaper in comparison.

Another problem is that sometimes public transport offers poor, slow service. For example, buses and trains stop frequently, which makes journeys slow. Also, there are bad links between buses and trains. Furthermore, there is often a lack of public transport in the countryside. One solution is for buses to have fast lanes on roads and to take fast routes without too many stops. Timetables should also be coordinated better. Some people think that country travellers should have cheaper fares.

Although there are many challenges in public transport, there are solutions and overall I think that public transport that is properly planned is a good thing.

Exercise 5: Correcting errors

a) This is another exercise where students have to use their editing skills. This time they are looking for specific mistakes. Go over the three examples and make sure they fully understand the mistakes highlighted. After you have looked at the third sentence, elicit other examples of incorrect parts of speech, e.g. using an adjective instead of an adverb.

b) Have students do the exercise individually and then check answers in pairs.

> **Typical mistakes:** Students often don't know where to start when editing their work. Therefore, it is a good idea for them to become familiar with common errors they make and look for these first. They can then do a second general check for sense and other mistakes.

Answers

... a major ~~causes~~ *cause* of air pollution ... number of flights ~~have~~ *has* increased ... pollution from air travel contributes ~~significant~~ *significantly* to climate change ... governments should spend ~~most~~ *more* money on scientific research ... different type of fuel which does not ~~harming~~ *harm* the environment They should find ways of travelling less as a ~~reduce~~ *reduction* in the number of journeys ...

Exercise 6: Identifying and correcting different types of mistakes

a) Draw attention to the Exam tip. Also point out that students need to have a clear understanding of their own weaknesses in order to edit effectively.

b) Have students complete the exercise individually and then check in pairs or groups.

> **Typical mistakes:** Students can be surprisingly vague about the kind of mistakes they make. This is a good opportunity to clarify exactly what kind of mistakes they make when they write. Use this opportunity to help the students identify their own specific areas of weakness.

Answers

1 e: cheap   2 a: forms   3 b: to charge   4 f: would / might / could / may   5 c: – (= zero article)   6 d: takes

Extension activity (50 mins)

Have students work in groups to discuss the text in Exercises 5 and 6. They should make notes on the text where they disagree with what the writer is saying, noting their own views. Then have them rewrite the text to express their own views.

Practice for the test (40 mins)

This can be done in class as pairwork or assigned for homework. Tell students to spend up to 40 minutes on the exercise, the time allotted in the exam. Remind them to look back at the Exam tips in the unit. Point out that students can do more activities online if they want extra practice or to consolidate what they have learnt.

Task 2

Model answer

Many countries in the world rely on motorways for speedy and efficient transportation as they are a very convenient way of travelling long distances. However, motorways also have negative aspects, such as dangerous traffic, damage to the environment and pollution. In this essay, I will look at some of the problems of motorways and how they can be overcome.

One major problem of motorways is that they can be dangerous. In many countries, the speed limit on motorways is very high. This means that any accidents are more likely to be serious and involve many vehicles. Sometimes in bad weather, several vehicles crash into each other and many people are killed or injured. This problem could be solved in a number of ways. People could have special lessons on how to drive safely on motorways. In addition, special signs could be displayed when driving conditions are bad to make people drive more slowly and safely. Alternatively, the general speed limit could be reduced slightly.

Secondly, motorways can spoil the environment. Motorways often go through beautiful areas and may damage plants and wildlife. This problem could be avoided by building motorways through less beautiful areas or putting some sections in tunnels. In addition, the large amount of traffic on motorways produces both air pollution and noise pollution. However, governments could help to reduce air pollution by making environmentally-friendly cars cheaper. Noise pollution could be reduced by changing motorway surfaces or by putting up soundproof fences.

Despite the problems of motorways, they are necessary and useful. With careful preparation and planning, the problems they cause could be reduced. People today are also more aware of environmental issues and as a result, cars and road transport in general are becoming more environmentally friendly.

Speaking: Facing life events

> **Student preparation for this class:** Have students complete the Online / Workbook language preparation exercises at home before the lesson begins.
>
> **Teacher preparation:** None

Online / Workbook language preparation

> **Focus:** These exercises introduce language for talking about important events: introducing words and phrases associated with important events; focusing on language to describe feelings; focusing on pronunciation: giving emphasis; focusing on grammar: comparing.

Develop your exam skills (Student's Book p. 112)

Focus: These exercises focus on using a range of grammar in Parts 1, 2 and 3 of the Speaking test. Exercises 1–4 focus on using the best tenses; Exercises 5–8 focus on tenses and grammatical phrases.

Introduction

Use Spot check 1 to recycle vocabulary connected with transport and reinforce the Online / Workbook language preparation. Use Spot check 2 to focus on gerunds and infinitives at an appropriate point in the lesson.

Spot check 1

To check students' use of adjectives to describe feelings (ending in -ed and -ing) and to revise vocabulary related to events and activities, do the following activity.

1. Put the words in bold on the board in a table as follows:

	boring	exciting	relaxing	tiring
event or activity	your cousin's graduation	getting your first job	doing yoga	learning to drive a car

2. Ask students to give you examples of events or activities that they have found boring, exciting, relaxing or tiring. Fill in an example on the board for each category, as shown above.

3. Ask students to work in pairs to add two more examples of their own in each column. Go round and check some of the answers.

4. Write the following on the board:

   What was it like when you got your first job? It was ...

   How do you feel when you do yoga? It makes me feel ...

5. Ask students the questions and make sure they understand the difference between *exciting* and *excited*, and *relaxing* and *relaxed*.

6. Ask students some more questions. They may have different answers: some may feel that yoga is boring, while others may think it is relaxing or tiring. Accept all answers that include an adjective with the correct ending.

7. Ask students to continue the exercise in pairs, using the examples they wrote in their own table.

Spot check 2

To check students' use of comparatives and superlatives and to revise vocabulary from previous units, do the following activity.

1. Ask students to give you three examples of each of the following categories: (1) sports, (2) healthy activities, (3) types of holidays, (4) jobs, (5) academic subjects, (6) types of TV programmes, (7) free time activities.

2. Write them in a table on the board, with the categories on the left, e.g.

(1) sports:	football	tennis	swimming
(2) healthy activities:	playing board games	eating healthy foods	doing sports

3. Dictate the following questions:

   a) Which sport is the most exciting? And the most tiring?

   b) Which job is the most interesting? And the most important?

   c) Which academic subject is the most interesting? And the most difficult?

   d) Which type of TV programme is the best? And the most boring?

   e) Which activity is the most difficult? And the most satisfying?

4. Ask a few students to answer the questions. They have to give an answer that is true for them. You could put the following prompt on the board to help students:

   ___ is more exciting than ___, but ___ is the most exciting.

   For example:

   Football is more exciting than swimming, but tennis is the most exciting.

   Tennis is more tiring than swimming, but football is the most tiring.

5. Ask students to choose three of the questions and to walk around the classroom to ask three other students a different question and to answer one of theirs. You can make this harder by removing the example sentences from the board.

Exercise 1: Correcting tenses in Part 1 answers

a) Draw the students' attention to the Exam information on page 112 and the Exam tip.

b) Ask students to follow the instructions and do the exercise individually.

c) You could follow up by eliciting a few more answers to questions using different tenses, e.g.

   Have you lived here for a long time?

   What are you studying at the moment?

   What are you going to do in the summer?

Answers

1 b – Answer a uses the present simple (*I play*) but the question is about events in the past. The answer has to include a past tense.

2 a – Answer b uses the present continuous (*I'm using*), which is used for actions happening at the time of speaking or temporary situations, but the question is about habits that are repeated in the present. The answer has to be in the present simple.
3 b – Answer a uses the present simple to talk about a period of time with *for*. The correct tense is the present perfect.

Exercise 2: Listening to identify tense
a) Play the recording (track 95) and ask students to listen carefully to identify the best beginning for the answers.
b) Help them distinguish between the pronunciation of *watch* and *watched* if necessary.

Answers
1 a **2** b **3** b **4** b **5** a

Exercise 3: Responding to Part 1 questions using an appropriate tense
Have students work in pairs for this exercise so that they can listen to each other's answers and discuss the tenses where necessary. If possible, have them record their answers.

> **Typical mistakes:** Students often use the present tense with a time indication in the past, e.g. *Yesterday, I go … .* Try to give them plenty of practice of past tenses, for example by asking them about their weekend. Before they answer, remind them to use appropriate tenses. You may want to use non-verbal ways to get them to self-correct when they use a present tense, e.g. by pulling your right hand towards your right shoulder a few times.

Exercise 4: Reading a Part 2 task card and identifying relevant grammar for the answer
Have students follow the instructions for the exercise and work in pairs to identify and discuss appropriate tenses.

Answers
past simple; *there was/were*; present perfect

Exercise 5: Using appropriate grammatical phrases and tenses in a Part 2 answer
a) Have students listen to the recording (track 96) and compare their answers in pairs.
b) If they have problems hearing the different tenses, go through the recording sentence by sentence, pausing it where appropriate and/or look at the audio script.

Answers
There are five: present simple; past simple; present perfect; *should*; *there was/were*

Exercise 6: Giving a Part 2 answer using appropriate tenses and grammatical phrases
a) Students could work in pairs, listening to and giving feedback for each other's answers. They should record their answers if possible.
b) Listen for common tense errors and address these with the class.

> **Typical mistakes:** Some students may make mistakes when using verbs with an irregular past form. If students need to learn some more irregular past forms, give them a list of irregular verbs (available in most grammar books) to study for homework, e.g. *do–did–done, begin–began–begun.*

Exercise 7: Identifying grammatical phrases and tenses in a Part 3 answer
Have students do the exercise individually and then compare answers in pairs.

Answers
1 have to **2** meet, is **3** more difficult **4** 're starting **5** 're going to

Exercise 8: Giving a Part 3 answer using a range of tenses and grammatical phrases
a) Draw attention to the Exam tip. Remind students that they will get better marks in the exam if they use a good range of grammatical structures and vocabulary.
b) Have students do the exercise in pairs so they can listen and give feedback to each other. They should record their answers if possible.

Extension activity (15 mins)
To provide further speaking opportunities and to practise using correct tense, do the following activity.

1. Ask students to work in groups of three. Give them some time to think about an exciting or funny event that happened to them at school. Tell them they will need to talk about it for two minutes. You could give them an example of your own, e.g. *When I was a pupil, I had a classmate who hid a teacher's books as a joke. The teacher's reaction was unusual. …*

2. Students take it in turns to tell their story. The other two students have to listen carefully and ask a follow-up question beginning with *what, when, how, where* or *why,* e.g. *How old were you when this happened? Why do you think the teacher didn't punish the student?*

Encourage them to help each other remember to use past tenses where appropriate.

Practice for the test (20–30 mins)

This can be done in class as pairwork or assigned for homework. Remind students to look back at the Exam tips in the unit. Point out that students can do more activities online if they want extra practice or to consolidate what they have learnt.

Part 1

Exercise 1
Model answers
1 Yes, I have a large family. There's my mother, my father, four brothers and one sister. My parents are from big families too, so I've got lots of cousins.

2 Yes, my favourite teacher at school was Mrs Holder. She was very kind and she taught English and French. Everybody enjoyed her lessons. She was clever and funny.

3 Yes, I'm a creative person so I enjoy making things. For example, I like drawing pictures or making cakes. I make lots of traditional food and I like eating out at restaurants.

4 My hometown is small. It's near the border and it's very pretty. There's a beach and a harbour. There aren't many shops or offices. It's very friendly and it's famous for the old bridge in the town centre.

5 I've been to lots of countries. I've been to Europe three or four times. I've been to America and I've been to Australia. I really enjoy travelling. I think it's important to learn about other countries.

Part 2

Exercise 2
Model answer
I'd like to describe an important event in my life. I'd like to describe my graduation from high school.

This took place in 2010 in my hometown. My father went to the the same school I did. My grandfather went to the school too and my mother taught there when I was young. It's important to my family. The graduation didn't happen at the school. It happened at the town hall. It's a beautiful, old building and it opens for special occasions.

My family were there. All of my friends from school were there. There were some important people from the town too. They made a speech and gave me my graduation certificate.

Finally, it was important to me for lots of different reasons. Firstly, my grandparents live in another town but they made the trip to see my graduation. I was surprised to see them. Secondly, I had extra tuition in my final year at school and it was very challenging for me. I felt really satisfied when I passed my exams. Finally, it was my birthday too, so I got lots of presents. It was one of the best days of my life.

Exercise 3
Model answers
1 Definitely. Life is very busy and it's important to remember special days. It's good to talk about it with your family and friends and look at photos of the event. It makes me feel very happy.

2 That's a difficult question. Let me think. I think planned events are more enjoyable because planned events are usually bigger and more important. For example, a graduation or a wedding.

Part 3

Exercise 4
Model answers
1 That's interesting. Let me see. Firstly, I think people are getting married when they are older now. People got married really young in my parents' generation. In my

opinion, I think organizing events is very different. Today we can plan things using the Internet at home, but in the past people spent lots of time travelling to shops or places to discuss events.

2 That's an interesting question. There are lots of ways to remember important events. I think people should remember the most important events by learning about the event and then going to a celebration each year. In my country, we have parades or festivals to remember important events. I think this is a good way.

3 In my country, sports and exams are very important. For example, there are lots of schools with special departments that teach sports. I think all schools organize lots of extra tuition to help students before exams. I had problems in my last year at school and I had extra classes to help me. It's important to work hard.

4 Yes, definitely. I've got lots of photos on my mobile and my laptop. They make me feel happy and they remind me of a special day or a funny day. It's one of the best ways to remember special occasions. Some people like making videos of the special occasion or buying gifts. I think these are good but in my opinion photos are the best.

Listening: Time management

Student preparation for this class: Have students complete the Online / Workbook vocabulary preparation exercises at home before the lesson begins.

Teacher preparation: None

Online / Workbook vocabulary preparation

Focus: The purpose of the exercises is to introduce vocabulary related to working, time management and study; provide practice in using punctuation correctly.

Develop your exam skills (Student's Book p. 114)

Focus: Exercises 1 and 2 focus on sentence completion questions in the Listening test, with a particular emphasis on listening out for the final s sound; Exercises 3 and 4 focus on completing a table.

Introduction
Use the Spot check to reinforce students' understanding of the Online / Workbook vocabulary preparation and review words for talking about work and time management.

Spot check
To reinforce working and time management vocabulary, do the following sorting activity.
1. Write all the words from Exercise 2 in the Workbook or Online in random order on the board.
2. Put students in pairs. Have them copy the words on the board into their notebooks, grouping the words as they do so. Do not tell them what the

groups should be. If there are any words which do not belong to any group, they can write them separately.

3. When students have finished, put two pairs together to see if they have grouped their words in the same way.

4. Ask students how they grouped their words in a whole class situation to check the meaning of the words.

 Exercise 1: Identifying correct sentences

a) Elicit ideas from students about what they need to check when doing sentence completion exercises. If necessary, remind them of the importance of writing grammatically correct sentences and not writing too many words.

b) Demonstrate the importance of using singular/plural and the third person *s* correctly. Write an example on the board: *My brothers sit on the sofa* and *My brother sits on the sofa*. Say each sentence while pointing to it. Highlight the similarity between *brothers sit* and *brother sits*, so they need to listen carefully for the *s* at the end of *sits* to be able to hear the difference. Then write: *My brother's friend is tall* to remind students about the possessive *s*.

c) Have students read the pairs of sentences and underline the differences between them before they listen. Put students in pairs and ask them to work together and say the differences between the singular form and plural form of the words: *lot* and *lots*, *class* and *classes* and so on.

d) Play the recording (track 100) and ask them to compare their answers.

Answers
1 b   **2** a   **3** b   **4** b

Typical mistakes: Students often put the possessive apostrophe in the wrong place, especially with plural nouns, as in *my sisters' children*. It might be easier to explain with a word that has a different plural spelling, for example *baby*. On the board, write *the baby's toys* and *the babies' toys* and ask students what the difference is.

 Exercise 2: Completing sentences

a) Play the recording (track 101) and let students compare their answers in pairs.

b) Have them check their answers carefully for grammar and punctuation errors and the incorrect use of singular or plural.

Answers
1 nine/9, five/5   **2** come into   **3** doesn't have   **4** On Mondays   **5** come out

Exercise 3: Understanding headings in a table

a) Draw students' attention to the second Exam tip on page 114. Point out that students may need to complete a table in the Listening test using headings that are given, but that in the recording they may hear different words with the same meaning.

b) Have students match the labels with alternative expressions. Remind them that they can guess the meaning of words they don't know. Have them compare their answers in pairs.

Answers
A 3   **B** 4   **C** 1   **D** 6   **E** 5   **F** 2

 Exercise 4: Completing headings in a table
Have students look at the table and think about it before they listen and then play the recording (track 102). Ask students to compare their answers.

Answers
1 B   **2** E   **3** F   **4** G   **5** A

Extension activity (20 mins)

1. To provide further practice in listening for the *s* sound, put students in pairs. Explain that they should write five pairs of sentences together in the singular and plural form. Give an example: *The cat likes to play in the garden* and *The cats like to play in the garden*. Monitor and help as students write their sentences together.

2. Rearrange the pairs so students work with a new partner. They should take it in turn to dictate their sentences to their new partner, who listens carefully and writes them down.

3. Students then check their sentences to make sure they wrote them correctly.

 Practice for the test (30 mins)

This can be done in class as pairwork or assigned for homework. Remind students to look back at the Exam tips in the unit. Point out that students can do more activities online or in their workbooks if they want extra practice or to consolidate what they have learnt.

Answers
1 and mental   **2** private   **3** flexible   **4** from home   **5** a year   **6** job sharing   **7** 27%   **8** work from home   **9** two small children   **10** her sister's

UNIT 12: MONEY

Listening: Spending habits

> **Student preparation for this class:** Have students complete the Online / Workbook vocabulary preparation exercises at home before the lesson begins.
>
> **Teacher preparation:** For the Spot check, make sets of cards with vocabulary items from Exercises 1 and 2 in the Workbook or Online (one word per card, sufficient for each group of three students. (15 mins)

Online / Workbook vocabulary preparation

> **Focus:** The purpose of the exercises is to introduce and practise vocabulary and collocations related to shopping; raises students' awareness of stressed words.

Develop your exam skills (Student's Book p. 116)

> **Focus:** These exercises review completing notes, multiple-choice questions and short-answer questions in the Listening test. They train students to listen for words which indicate the structure of a talk, practise answering multiple-choice questions and analyse short answers.

Introduction

1   Introduce the unit by getting students to talk about the pictures on pages 118, 121 and 122 in pairs. Ask them to talk about what they can see and how it relates to the unit topic, *Money*, and the Listening section, *Spending habits*. Recycle some of the shopping and spending vocabulary from the Online / Workbook preparation by discussing students' spending habits.

2   Use the Spot check to reinforce students' understanding of the Online / Workbook vocabulary preparation and recycle words connected with shopping and spending.

Spot check

To reinforce the shopping vocabulary in Exercises 1 and 2 in the Workbook or Online, do the following activity.

1.   Put students into groups of three and hand out a set of cards to each group.

2.   Ask one student in each group to shuffle the cards and place them face down on the table.

3.   Students take it in turns to pick a card, but they must not show it to the other members of their group. The student must get the others to guess the word on the card by giving them clues, e.g. *This shop sells lots of different things.*

4.   The student who guesses correctly keeps the card. Then the next person chooses a card and play continues.

5.   The student with the most cards wins.

   Repeat the game if necessary to help students gain fluency in this topic area.

 ### Exercise 1: Predicting words to complete gapped notes
a)   Have students predict the missing words and compare their ideas in pairs or groups. Remind them that they should always try to guess what they will hear before they hear it. This will be good preparation for when the recording is played.

b)   Play the recording (track 106) so that students can check and amend their answers.

Answers
1 75%   **2** 60%   **3** 50%   **4** supermarkets   **5** markets   **6** small shops

 ### Exercise 2: Multiple-choice questions with more than one answer
a)   Draw students' attention to the second Exam tip on page 116. Suggest that they underline the number of correct answers so that they do not choose too many or too few.

b)   Ask students to guess the answers and then compare their answers.

c)   Play the recording (track 107) and let them compare their answers in pairs. Play the recording a second time so they can check their answers.

Answers
a, c, e

Exercise 3: Identifying problems with short answers
a)   Draw students' attention to the Exam tip again.

b)   Ask students to complete the exercise individually and then compare their answers in pairs.

> **Typical mistakes:** Students may confuse short-answer questions with sentence completion questions. Short-answer questions do not need a full grammatical sentence; sentence completion questions do need to form a full grammatically accurate sentence. Point this out to students and remind them of the differences each time you come across these two task types.

Answers
1 a   **2** b   **3** d   **4** c

Extension activity (20 mins)
To provide further practice in listening for information about shopping and making notes, ask students to work in groups of four to listen and talk about their shopping habits. Have students make notes in preparation for talking about their shopping habits. Give them ten

minutes to prepare for their talk. Monitor and help with language.

1. Have students take it in turns to talk about where they like to go shopping, who with, when they like to go and what they like to buy.

2. Ask other students to listen carefully and make notes as they listen.

3. The students who listened should then compare their notes with each other and check that they understood the same things.

4. The next student should then give their talk in the same way.

5. This continues until every student has given their talk.

Practice for the test (30 mins)

This can be done in class as pairwork or assigned for homework. Remind students to look back at the Exam tips in the unit. Point out that students can do more activities online if they want extra practice or to consolidate what they have learnt.

Answers
1 (more) mature people   2 spending patterns   3 up to 30   4 over 55   5–7 (in any order) f, a, d   8 cars and computers   9 beauty treatments   10 young men

Speaking: Possessions

> **Student preparation for this class:** Have students complete the Online / Workbook language preparation exercises at home before the lesson begins.
>
> **Teacher preparation:** If you decide to do the Extension activity, you will need to download and print a copy of the handout for each student. (2 mins)

Online / Workbook language preparation

> **Focus:** These exercises introduce language for talking about possessions: introducing words and phrases to describe objects; focusing on language to describe objects; focusing on pronunciation: linking words; focusing on grammar: present perfect with *for* and *since*.

Develop your exam skills (Student's Book p. 118)

> **Focus:** These exercises give tips and offer practice in a range of skills that are necessary in Parts 1, 2 and 3 of the Speaking test. Exercises 1 and 2 focus on fluency and coherence; Exercises 3 and 4 focus on using a range of grammar; Exercises 5 and 6 focus on using a range of vocabulary.

Introduction

Use Spot check 1 to recycle language for talking about possessions from the Workbook / Online language preparation. Use Spot checks 2 and 3 at appropriate stages of the lesson.

> **Spot check 1**
>
> To check students' recall of phrases for describing objects, do the following activity.
>
> 1. Have students do Exercise 5 from the Workbook or Online again, but for another object they own and like.
>
> 2. Ask students to read the description they wrote in Exercise 8, and the phrases from Exercise 6 again.
>
> 3. Put students in groups of 3–4. With books closed, have them describe both of their objects to the rest of the group. They describe the object they wrote about at home and the one they have just written notes about. They should be careful not to name the objects. The others have to guess what the objects are.

> **Spot check 2**
>
> To check students' ability to link words, do the following activity.
>
> 1. Ask a few students from each group to volunteer to repeat one of the descriptions from Spot check 1 for the whole group without naming the object. Draw their attention to the *Watch Out!* box in the Workbook or Online before they start.
>
> 2. Pay attention to the way they link their consonant and vowel sounds, give feedback and, if necessary, further practice (say and repeat).

> **Spot check 3**
>
> To check students' ability to use the present perfect with *for* and *since*, do the following activity.
>
> 1. Ask students to stay in their groups. Write the following questions on the board:
>
>   *a) What important object have you owned since you were a child?* OR *b) What object have you wanted since you were little?*
>
>   *a) What object have you used for years?* OR *b) What object have you only had for a short while?*
>
> 2. Have students ask each other one a) question and one b) question. Ask them to start their answers with *I* and to use *for* or *since* in their sentences, e.g. *I've had my first school bag since I was six. I've wanted a TV in my bedroom since I was little. I've used my travel bag for years. I've had my new phone for two days now.*
>
>   Make sure students are using the present perfect correctly.

Exercise 1: Completing tips on how to develop fluency and coherence

a) Draw students' attention to the Exam information on page 118. Make sure they are clear about the different assessment areas; you could write them on the board.

b) Explain or ask questions to elicit that Exercise 1 gives tips for developing fluency and coherence.

c) Have students do the exercise individually and then check their answers in pairs.

Answers
1 pause, natural   **2** notes   **3** organize

Exercise 2: Giving fluent and coherent answers to Part 2 answers
a) Have students read the task card and elicit how they can plan their answers (make notes on what they want to say and plan phrases to organize it).
b) Get students to record their answers if possible. Ask them to work in pairs to listen to each other's answers and give feedback about the notes and the useful phrases they wrote down. They should also say whether they thought the delivery was at a natural pace.

Exercise 3: Completing tips on how to develop grammatical accuracy and range
a) Ask students to explain which assessment area these tips are for (grammatical accuracy and range).
b) Have students do the exercise individually and then check their answers in pairs.

Answers
1 tenses   **2** carefully, choose

Exercise 4: Giving grammatically accurate answers to Part 3 questions
a) Have students read the questions and elicit what they should think about (the grammar they want to use and the grammar in the question).
b) Get students to record their answers if possible. Ask them to work in pairs to listen to each other's answers and give feedback on the accuracy and range of the grammar.

Exercise 5: Completing tips on how to develop accuracy and range of vocabulary
a) Ask students to say which assessment area these tips are for (accuracy and range of vocabulary).
b) Have students do the exercise individually and then check their answers in pairs.

Answers
1 topic   **2** repeat, describing   **3** similar, adverbs

Exercise 6: Giving answers to Part 2 using a range of vocabulary
a) Have students read the task card and elicit what they should think about (the vocabulary they want to use and how to avoid repeating words).
b) Get students to record their answers if possible. Ask them to work in pairs to listen to each other's answers and give feedback on whether they used a good range of vocabulary.

> **Typical mistakes:** Some students may take a long time to decide which photograph they should describe. Tell them that they are wasting useful time if they do not make a quick decision. Advise them to think of photographs that are related to vocabulary topics they

> are confident about, e.g. if they are good at talking about possessions or holidays, they should think of photographs that relate to one of these topics.

Extension activity (15 mins)
To provide further speaking opportunities and to raise students' awareness of their strengths and weaknesses in grammar, vocabulary, fluency and pronunciation, do the following activity.

1. Have students work with a different partner. Ask them to listen to each other's answers for one of the questions from Exercise 6 in the Student's Book (live or on the recording they made) and complete the grid (see handout). They should put a tick (✓) in the *Yes* column if something has been done well, or a tick in the *Not always* column if something could be improved.

2. Students work together on tips to help improve any problem areas, e.g. *Practise saying* /θ/ or /ð/ *rather than* /t/. Try not to let intonation go up at the end of sentences. They swap handouts at the end of the activity so that they can take home their own tips.

 ## Practice for the test (20–30 mins)

This can be done in class as pairwork or assigned for homework. Remind students to look back at the Exam tips in the unit. Point out that students can do more activities online if they want extra practice or to consolidate what they have learnt.

Part 1

Exercise 1
Model answers
1 I'm from China. My hometown is Beijing. I've lived there since I was a baby.
2 The most popular place to go shopping in my hometown is the shopping mall near the stadium. It's really big and has lots of different shops and cafés.
3 I rarely shop online. I like going to shops and looking at things. I sometimes buy music online.
4 I bought a present for my best friend last week. I bought her a silver necklace for her birthday. She was very surprised.
5 I like visiting galleries and museums. I really enjoy meeting friends for coffee and chatting. It's very relaxing.

Part 2

Exercise 2
Model answer
I'd like to describe something that is very important to me. This possession is my mobile phone.

It's very small, modern and red and silver. I think it's made of metal and plastic. It looks great. It's very fashionable and expensive too. I carry it in my bag every day.

I've had it for six months. I got it when I was on holiday in England. It reminds me of my holiday and the rainy weather. I've used it every day since I bought it. I use it to download apps and listen to music. I text or call my family with it. I can use the Internet and I can organize my diary. I can do everything with it. It's really good.

Finally, it's important to me because it's my connection with my family. Now I'm living and studying in another country, I rarely see my family. I can make video calls with my phone and see my parents. It makes me feel happy.

Exercise 3
Model answers
1 Yes, there are lots of mobile phones in shops. I can go to the shopping mall tomorrow and buy a new mobile phone. I enjoy shopping so it would be fun.
2 Yes, absolutely. I think my mobile phone is one of the best phones. My best friend likes my mobile because it's smaller than his mobile phone.

Part 3

Exercise 4
Model answers
1 That's an interesting question. It depends. I think possessions can make people happy, yes. For example, you're working really hard for your exams and then someone buys you a good luck present. I think that would make people happy. Lots of people own expensive objects but they feel sad. In my opinion, I think friends and family make people happier than objects.
2 My most important possession is probably my mobile phone. I always carry it in my bag and I use it every day. I think my parents' important possessions are probably big things like cars or houses. I think family photos are probably more important to my mother. I suppose young people think modern, electrical things are more important than big, expensive objects.
3 Yes, absolutely. I love shopping. It's a relaxing activity for me and I spend lots of my free time going to the shopping mall. It's relaxing because you can meet your friends and go shopping together. I like shopping online too. When the shopping mall is very busy or when you're really tired, you can look online and then buy things.
4 That's interesting. Let me see. I really enjoy giving presents to people. I like thinking about the present, buying it and wrapping it. When the person opens the present, it makes me feel satisfied. But I like getting presents too. I got this coat for my birthday and I've worn it every day since my birthday. I think it's better to receive a present.

Writing: Money and happiness

Student preparation for this class: Have students complete the Online / Workbook language preparation exercises at home before the lesson begins.

Teacher preparation: Download and photocopy the handout for Spot check 1 (one copy for each pair of students). Download, photocopy and cut up the handout for Spot check 2 (one copy for each student). (15 mins)

Online / Workbook language preparation

Focus: The purpose of these exercises is to introduce common words used to talk about personal finance; introduce the use of pronouns for reference within a text.

Develop your exam skills (Student's Book p. 120)

Focus: These exercises train students to write opinion essays that include a range of opinions, including the writer's, in preparation for writing one of the question types in Task 2.

Introduction

Use Spot check 1 to recycle vocabulary and collocations from the Online / Workbook language preparation connected with finance. Use Spot check 2 before doing Exercise 6, or at an appropriate stage of the lesson.

Spot check 1
1. Remind students how words are used together in different kinds of collocations or other clusters, e.g. 'verb + noun' or 'noun + noun'.
2. Put students in pairs. Then give each pair a copy of the Spot check 1 handout. They have to match the words from Exercises 1 and 2 in the Workbook or Online with each 'brain teaser'.

(Answers: **1** wealth, possessions **2** rich, wealthy **3** save, spend **4** wealth, poverty **5** savings, income **6** tax, income, salary, wealth, savings **7** salary, income)

Spot check 2
To provide further practice in using reference within a text, put students in groups of four to match corresponding sentences.

1. Give each student a copy of the Spot check 2 handout.
2. Nominate one student in each group to say their first sentence. The student who has the corresponding second sentence reads it out. Continue in a clockwise direction.
3. Have students discuss what they think of each sentence, e.g. whether they agree or disagree or have some experience of their own.

(Answers: **1** d **2** c **3** h **4** a **5** f **6** g **7** b **8** e)

Exercise 1: Language for introducing opinions
a) Go over the Exam information on writing opinion essays. Ask questions, e.g.

Why should you include a range of opinions in your essay even though it asks for your opinion?

How does this link with what you learnt in Unit 7 about writing advantages and disadvantages?

What verbs can be used to introduce your own opinion?

What about other people's opinions?

b) Ask students to do the exercise following the instructions in the book and then compare their answers in pairs. Discuss the variety of phrases that introduce opinions in class feedback.

c) Follow up by asking students if they identify more with the writer's opinions, other opinions or if they don't identify with one more than the other.

> **Typical mistakes:** Students often fail to use a range of vocabulary in their essays. Point out the importance of using a variety of verb phrases in their writing and that this is an easy way to gain marks.

Answers
1 <u>According to</u> the government, traditional families are the happiest. OPO
2 There are many things that can make people happy. <u>In my view</u>, family and friends are the most important. WO
3 <u>Some teachers believe</u> that children should learn how to manage money at school. They suggest that this could help the economy in the future. OPO
4 <u>I believe</u> that the government should provide more financial help to poor families. WO
5 <u>My personal opinion is</u> that having an enjoyable job is essential for happiness. WO
6 <u>Many people argue</u> that all citizens should pay as little tax as possible. OPO
7 <u>I think</u> that wealthy people should pay more tax. WO
8 <u>Parents often claim</u> that they need more money. OPO

Exercise 2: Identifying phrases for introducing opinions
a) Draw attention to the Exam tip. Point out that it should be clear from the start what the writer thinks – students will see this in the introduction they are about to read. Refer to the Grammar section: *Phrases to introduce opinions.*

b) Have students do the exercise individually and then check answers in pairs.

c) Highlight in feedback how the writer states a general opinion at the beginning, goes on to say what others think, and then clearly states his/her own opinion.

Answers
… <u>Some people say that</u> having more money … while <u>other people argue that</u> happiness can … <u>In my view</u>, …
1 that having more money makes life less stressful
2 that happiness can be found in other aspects of life, such as work, family or hobbies
3 that having more money does not make people happier but it makes life easier
4 two reasons

Exercise 3: Writing an introduction to an opinion essay
Go through the instructions carefully and make sure students understand that they can add their own opinions to the notes provided, i.e. the notes are just there to help. Point out that the exam question has very similar wording to the one in Exercise 2 so they can use that introduction as a model.

Model answer
Personal happiness can come from many different aspects of life. For some people happiness comes from being successful, either at work or at school or within a community. On the other hand, some people argue that personal happiness depends on being able to enjoy life and on having a positive attitude when bad things happen. I believe that personal happiness is more about individual personality and less about particular life events, personal success or possessions.

Exercise 4: Using linking words that introduce agreement and contrast
a) Draw attention to the Exam tip. Remind students that they dealt with these linking words in Unit 8. Then introduce Exercise 4, pointing out that the gapped paragraph follows on from the one in Exercise 2, i.e. it gives the first reason for the writer's opinion.

b) Have students complete the paragraph in small groups. There are several answers for each gap, so encourage students to discuss their answers fully so that they feel comfortable about how they are used.

Answers
1 Also / In addition / Similarly / Furthermore / Moreover
2 although   **3** However / On the other hand   **4** Also / In addition   **5** However / On the other hand

Exercise 5: Developing notes and writing a paragraph for an opinion essay
Have students work individually to complete the second paragraph. First, they have to extend the notes and then write the paragraph. Point out that they should express views that follow naturally from paragraph 1.

Model answer
Secondly, having more money can help people plan for the future so they have more control over their lives. I believe that saving money helps people to become more independent because they will not have to ask for financial help when they are old. In addition, they can plan for things like their children's education or buying a bigger house. However, people with little money cannot plan for the future easily because they have to focus on the present. Some people argue that having less money does not prevent people planning for the future, but in my view, it makes it much more difficult.

Exercise 6: Using referencing words in an opinion essay
a) Have students complete the gapped paragraph individually.

b) During class feedback establish the kind of opinions being expressed, i.e. that you have to find happiness in yourself. Discuss what kind of second paragraph such a person might write. Highlight that it should complement the first paragraph. Elicit possible extensions:

- Extend one of the examples mentioned of the 'good things in their life': family, friends, good health, or pets.

- Bring in another more general point: enjoying small things, helping others, etc.

Answers
1 this 2 They 3 also 4 However / On the other hand
5 this / it 6 These / Such 7 These 8 but / although

Exercise 7: Writing an additional paragraph for an opinion essay

Have students write the second paragraph individually and ask them to compare their paragraphs with a partner.

> **Typical mistakes:** Many students find it difficult to contrast ideas or make connections between them. This is a skill that can be learnt if they are given regular practice. One way to do this is to ask students to read an article and identify the opinion of the writer. Then ask them to think about what other views the same writer might have.

Model answer

Enjoying the little things in life can be another important factor in happiness. Some people think that life is about achieving great things like having a successful job and a big house, but life is also about small pleasures like having a good dinner or a nice walk in the countryside. If people enjoyed these little things more, then they might be happier in general.

Practice for the test (50 mins)

This can be done in class as pairwork or assigned for homework. Remind students to look back at the Exam tips in the unit. Point out that students can do more activities online if they want extra practice or to consolidate what they have learnt.

Task 2

Model answer

Everybody wants to be happy, but there is often a debate over what makes a person happy. Some people believe happiness can only come from friends and family. According to other people, happiness comes from money and possessions. I believe that happiness comes both from close family and friends and also from having enough money and possessions.

Firstly, everybody needs enough money to live – to pay for a home, food and other necessities. If people have money to spare after paying for these things, they often spend it on possessions that make them feel happy for a short time. However, this kind of happiness often does not last because money and possessions alone cannot bring happiness. Rich people can be very lonely if they don't share their money and possessions with others. It has also been proved that having a good time with friends and family brings people more happiness than a fast car or new clothes.

On the other hand, very poor people are not usually happy even if they have large families and many friends. Money worries cause them a lot of stress and this means they are not able to enjoy life. Their friends and family may be able to support them and help them by lending them money, but this may lead to problems. I agree that family and friends are important, but without a good income, they may not be enough.

In conclusion, I believe that both money and possessions as well as a family and friends are important to happiness and that neither is more important than the other. People who don't have enough money to live but who have good friends and a strong family may be just as unhappy as wealthy people who have more than enough but no family or friends to share it with.

Reading: Running a business

> **Student preparation for this class:** Have students complete the Online / Workbook language preparation exercises at home before the lesson begins.
>
> **Teacher preparation:** For the Extension activity, source a reading text on a business topic of an appropriate level of difficulty (200–300 words). Photocopy the text so that there is one copy for each group of students. Cut up the text into individual paragraphs. (30 minutes)

Online / Workbook language preparation

> **Focus:** The purpose of these exercises is to introduce words relating to money and banks; focus on commonly confused words for quantities: *few* and *a few*.

Develop your exam skills (Student's Book p. 123)

> **Focus:** These exercises train students to find and recognize sections of a text that have specific functions, including topic sentences, explanations and examples.

Introduction

Use the Spot check to recycle vocabulary from the Online / Workbook language preparation relating to money and spending.

Spot check
To reinforce vocabulary related to money, do the following activity.
1. Put students in three teams and give each team one of the following categories: things that you can do in a bank (e.g. open a savings account), things that you have to pay (e.g. rent) and ways to get money (e.g. withdraw money from the cashpoint).
2. Each team has two minutes to write a list of as many things as they can that fit into their category.
3. Teams take turns to read out their list. The other teams guess what the category is.
4. The teams can then add more ideas to the other teams' lists.

Exercise 1: Identifying the function of information in different parts of a text

a) Go over the Exam information on matching information and also draw attention to the Exam tip.

Check that students are familiar with the headings in the box by giving or asking for examples of the different functions, e.g. *this will happen if* = condition.

b) Have students skim the text before they do the exercise individually. They then check their answers in pairs.

c) Follow up by asking them what features of the language helped them decide on their answers.

Answers

explanation (x 2)	the companies that are quoted in the leading share price indices small and medium-sized enterprises, with less than 250 employees
reason (x 3)	successive governments have sought to encourage small business start-ups forcing entrepreneurs to go through planning steps to make sure their business propositions are viable to make sure that planned products and services meet customer needs
example	new and developing small businesses
comparison	this is up from the previous year and represents the best figures ever recorded
condition	if new entrepreneurs are to succeed, if new businesses are to thrive

Exercise 2: Identifying paragraph topics and topic sentences

a) Ask questions to check that students understand what a topic sentence is. Then have them do the exercise individually, following the instructions in the book.

b) Students check their answers in pairs or groups and give reasons for their choice.

Answers
1 Paragraph A: c   2 Paragraph D: b   3 Paragraph E: b

Exercise 3: Finding key words and ideas in a text

a) Have students underline the key words in the questions and compare their ideas in groups. They should check their choice of key words against the answer key before looking for the answers in the text individually.

b) Draw their attention to the Glossary box under the reading passage and remind them that skimming the text will ensure they don't miss any boxes like this in the exam.

c) Encourage students to discuss their answers in groups.

Answers
1 Which paragraph mentions statistics? B
2 In paragraph A, which word indicates that the text will not be about large businesses? *However*
3 In paragraph C, which sentence explains why new and developing small businesses are crucial to the success of the economy? *Behind the policy is a belief that small businesses contribute to a stronger economic base, and that they have the ability to thrive in a competitive global business environment.*
4 Which paragraph builds on the same idea as the one in A and C (mentioned in question 3)? D

Extension activity (30 mins)

To provide further practice in identifying key information in paragraphs, have students analyse the texts that you prepared before the class.

1. Students work in groups of 4–5. Hand out the cut-up paragraphs to each group.

2. Have each group work together to put the paragraphs into the correct order.

3. They then decide on the function of each paragraph and think about what helped them order the paragraphs.

Practice for the test (30 mins)

This can be done in class as pairwork or assigned for homework. Remind students to look back at the Exam tips in the unit. Point out that students can do more activities online if they want extra practice or to consolidate what they have learnt.

Answers
1 B   2 F   3 I   4 C   5 G   6 E

PRACTICE TEST ANSWER KEY

Listening

Section 1

1 a **2** b **3** a **4** 4, The Willows **5** 07632 112254
6 19th June **7** £360 **8** garden centre **9** school
10 vegetable

Section 2

11 everyday inventions **12** half an hour / 30 minutes
13 ground floor **14** C **15** B **16** B **17** A **18** film title
19 (little) calendar **20** number of tickets

Section 3

21 (student) accommodation **22** distance from campus
23 public transport **24–26** (in any order) b, e, f
27 16% **28** near bus stop **29** 20% **30** 54%

Section 4

31 look for food **32** feed their young / find extra food
33 the tropics **34** warmer climates **35** spring / it comes
earlier **36** food available earlier / higher temperatures
37 population / (it) drops drastically **38** D **39** F **40** B

Speaking

Part 1

Model answers

1 I'm a student. I'm studying medicine and I'm in my
second year at university. And I study English too. It's my
favourite subject.

2 No, I'm an only child, so I don't have any brothers or
sisters. But I have lots of cousins and aunts and uncles
because my parents have lots of brothers and sisters.
I have three nephews too.

3 My hometown is very big. It's busy and dirty. There are
lots of cars and there's lots of traffic. But the people are
really friendly and it's a good city for tourists. You can go
to the beach, you can go shopping or you can eat in a
traditional restaurant.

4 It's always hot and sunny. I think tourists enjoy the
weather. We have a rainy season and this lasts for about
two months. I don't like the rainy season because it
makes me feel sad.

5 In my country, football is very popular and it's my
favourite hobby. I love playing football with my friends.
We play in competitions every weekend. I enjoy watching
sports programmes on TV too. I also like going to the gym
or going jogging, but sometimes I like doing nothing or
watching films with my cousins. It's important to relax.

Part 2

Model answer

I'd like to describe a person who helped me. I'm going to
talk about a teacher from my high school. Her name was
Mrs White.

I met Mrs White on my first day at school. I felt very
nervous because I didn't know anyone. My family moved
to the city about one month before the school term
started, so I didn't have any friends. Mrs White talked to
my parents and then we walked to her classroom. I sat at
a table with two funny boys. We've been friends since my
first day.

Mrs White was a kind, friendly person. She always
listened to students and helped them. She was a great
teacher and her lessons were interesting. She made me
feel confident about studying. I think she was special
because she liked everybody in her class. She encouraged
us to work hard and to think about jobs and careers. But
she was really funny and the class had fun too.

Finally, Mrs White helped me because she encouraged
me to apply for a university course. She helped me with
my application form and she organized a scholarship for
me. She was great.

Yes, I'd like to help someone in this way. I think it's
important to help others. Actually, I'm training to be a
teacher, so I'm going to help lots of children. I'm going to
graduate in the summer and then I'm going to work in a
school in my hometown. I'm very excited.

Part 3

Model answers

1 Yes, definitely. In my opinion, we can learn lots of
things from older generations. Firstly, we can learn about
history or tradition and what happened in the past.
Secondly, we can listen to advice from people with lots of
experience. Finally, I think it's important to listen to a
different opinion because it helps us to understand the
world.

2 That's an interesting question. Let me think. I think
today's families rarely live together. People live and work
all over the world. Families often don't live in the same
town or country. I'm not sure, but I think families lived
together in the past. In my opinion, I think it was easier
for families to help family members in the past. It's
harder when people live in another place.

3 That's a very difficult question. I'm not sure. I think
families should help, but we should be independent too.
It depends. I think we should ask families for help with
big problems because they can give advice or money. But
I think we should try being independent with smaller
problems.

4 In my country, there's a coming-of-age ceremony on our eighteenth birthday. This is when a person becomes an adult. It's a very important occasion and we celebrate it with family and friends. But I think some people become adults after they are eighteen. For example, when you are independent and live in another country, or when you get married.

Reading

Reading passage 1

1 YES **2** NOT GIVEN **3** YES **4** YES **5** NO **6** YES

7 A **8** A **9** B **10** B **11** b **12** a **13** d **14** b

Reading passage 2

15 vii **16** vi **17** iii **18** i **19** v **20** iii **21** i

22 viii **23** vi **24** solution **25** advertising

26 extensions **27** chip

Reading passage 3

28 at the weekend **29** parking further / parking further away **30** life not regular/ not as regular

31 do some skipping / do skipping **32** outdoors

33 run / a run **34** F **35** B **36** D **37** a calmer style

38 (your) local council **39** TRUE **40** NOT GIVEN

Writing

Task 1

Model answer

The bar chart shows the sales of four different types of music across five age ranges in 2010 in the USA. The youngest age group is 16–22-year-olds and the oldest is the over 58-year-olds.

Different music genres were popular with different age ranges. Overall, young people between the ages of 16 and 31 preferred to buy rock and pop music, whereas older people liked jazz and classical music. We can see that rock music was the most popular music genre for three out of five age groups. In all age groups except the 46–57-year-olds and the over 58-year-olds, jazz sold more recordings than classical.

Some age groups preferred to buy a specific genre of music. For example, the over-58 group bought approximately four and a half million classical recordings, the 23–31 age group bought just over four million rock recordings in 2010, and the youngest group bought almost five million pop recordings. Sales of rock recordings were the highest of all the genres in 2010.

Task 2

Model answer

Nowadays, the Internet is used widely in education around the world. Some people say it is beneficial for teaching and learning because there is so much information available. However, others claim that the Internet is bad for students' research skills and believe that its use should be restricted. I believe that use of the Internet should be limited in some ways, but it is still a valuable educational tool.

Firstly, the Internet is essential for many people today. It is widely used in the workplace and people's everyday lives, both for finding information, for personal finance, for keeping in touch with friends and family, for social networking, and so on. Therefore, school students should learn how to use it correctly. In addition, students also need it for research in school and university subjects. Nowadays the most up-to-date information can be found on the Internet rather than in books, which can become out of date very quickly. Using the Internet is a convenient way of finding out information and developing independent research skills.

However, the Internet has some negative aspects. For example, not all websites are reliable or contain accurate information. Students need to learn how to evaluate and check the material they find on the Internet. Also, many students simply copy large amounts of material such as essays from the Internet. Some students then pretend that this material is their own work, which is illegal. If students simply copy information or material from the Internet without understanding or analysing it, they will not learn it fully. Teachers need to teach students how to research and use information from the Internet properly.

In conclusion, schools and universities should teach students how to use the Internet by teaching them good research skills. If students know how to use the Internet effectively, they are likely to become better students and have better employment opportunities in the future.